D0569815

MARK TWAIN

TWAIN

FOR

CAT

LOVERS

Mark Twain with close friend at his last home, Stormfield.
PHOTO COURTESY: KEVIN MAC DONNELL

MARK TWAIN ℔ CAT LOVERS

True and Imaginary Adventures
WITH FELINE FRIENDS

Edited by
MARK DAWIDZIAK

GUILFORD, CONNECTICUT

An imprint of Rowman & Littlefield

Distributed by NATIONAL BOOK NETWORK

British Library Cataloguing in Publication Information Available

Library of Congress Cataloging-in-Publication Data Available

ISBN 978-1-4930-1957-1 (cloth)
ISBN 978-1-4930-2709-5 (e-book)

♾™ The paper used in this publication meets the minimum requirements of American National Standard for Information Sciences—Permanence of Paper for Printed Library Materials, ANSI/NISO Z39.48-1992.

FOR SARA,

who has shared the love and the laughter,

along with many Twain travels

and the company of (so far) six cats

CONTENTS

INTRODUCTION viii
Mark Twain in the Company of Cats

PART I. 1
Cats Who Eat Cocoanuts, Smoke Cigars, and Get Blown Up

   1. The Cat Who Swallowed the Painkiller 2
   2. The Cat Who Went Out on a Limb 11
   3. The Cat Who Howled at a Fiddle 21
   4. The Cat Who Blowed Up. 23
   5. The Cat Who Ate Cocoanuts 31
   6. The Cat Who Conquered an Elephant. 38
   7. The Cat Who Smoked Cigars 40
   8. The Cat Who Haunted Westminster Abbey 42

PART II. 47
No Home Complete Without a Cat

   9. The Cat and the Burglar Alarm. 48
  10. Papa Is Particularly Fond of Cats. 50
  11. The Cat in the Ruff. 53
  12. "A Cat-Tale" 57
  13. Satan and Sin 71
  14. Fast Asleep . . . Wide Awake 73
  15. Sour Mash, Sackcloth, and Ashes. 78
  16. Understanding Cat Language. 88
  17. A Feline Royal Family 91
  18. Home Is Where the Cat Is 94

PART III. 97
Give Me a Cat

  19. The Cat as a Learning Tool 98
  20. Praise for a German Cat. 100
  21. The Kittens of Great Falls, Montana 101

22. A Cat Who Gets Around 105
23. Undermining the Moral Fiber of a Cat. 107
24. A Place a Cat Would Like. 109
25. Bambino. 112
26. Discipline "Don't Apply" to a Cat 129
27. The Cat Came Loafing In. 131
28. A Cat's Opinion on Pain. 133
29. The Cat in the Corner Pocket 136
30. The Shakespearean Cat. 141

PART IV. **145**
What Is Dead Cats Good For?

31. Warts Follow Cat 146
32. Cat Calls. 149
33. The Naturalist Tavern 151

PART V. **155**
Lions and Tigers and Twain

34. The Lion of St. Mark 156
35. Lunch for a Lion? 159
36. Tiger on the Front Porch 163
37. The Tiger Cub. 164

PART VI. **167**
No Ordinary Cats

38. The Lucky Cat. 168
39. No Orthodox Cat 179
40. A Fable 182

ACKNOWLEDGMENTS **186**

ABOUT THE EDITOR **188**

INTRODUCTION

Mark Twain in the Company of Cats

I t is no great leap to suppose that the animal most asso-
ciated with Mark Twain is a frog . . . a celebrated jumping frog, in fact. "It certainly had a wide celebrity," he
observed, and that assessment is, if anything, an exercise in
understatement. There is a poster advertising an early Mark
Twain lecture appearance, and it shows the writer riding that
frog, horseback style, as it sails over a fence. The image is as
symbolic as it is delightful. Mark Twain did, indeed, ride the
success of his 1865 humorous tale "Jim Smiley and His Jumping Frog" (later "The Celebrated Jumping Frog of Calaveras
County") to a national reputation. But as much as Mark Twain
owed to that uncommonly fine frog, cats were the animals that
held the highest place in his regard and his affections. He loved
cats, compliments, and cigars, and no day would have been
judged truly complete for him without a generous supply of
all three.

It is unquestionably true that the writer born Samuel
Langhorne Clemens in 1835 found delight and inspiration in
all kinds of animals, from camels and coyotes to mules and

monkeys. Indeed, that jumping frog cleared the way for hilarious tales about a horse billed as a Genuine Mexican Plug, as well as an idiotic ant, a deceitful turkey, an impudent crow, a pious chameleon, and a determined blue jay, just to name a few of the animal stars in Mark Twain's world. "Animals were integral to Mark Twain's work as a writer from the first story that earned him national renown to pieces he wrote during his final years that remained unpublished at his death," Mark Twain scholar Shelley Fisher Fishkin noted in the opening of her engaging and insightful collection *Mark Twain's Book of Animals.*

"From the beginning to the end of his long career Mark Twain not only lived in this animal kingdom but he also rejoiced in it—he celebrated it," wrote author and critic Maxwell Geismar in the introduction to his book, *The Higher Animals: A Mark Twain Bestiary.* "While his view of mankind may have changed with the tragic wisdom of age," Geismar said, "his pleasure in his animal friends remained constant."

Yet the animal most integral to his life—the one rejoiced in and celebrated to the greatest degree—was the cat. Susy Clemens summed it up in the biography of her famous father that she started at the age of thirteen: "The difference between papa and mama is, that mama loves morals and papa loves cats."

Cats scamper throughout many of his books, including *The Innocents Abroad, Roughing It, The Adventures of Tom Sawyer, Life on the Mississippi, A Tramp Abroad, A Connecticut Yankee in King Arthur's Court, Pudd'nhead Wilson, Following the Equator, Tom Sawyer Abroad,* and his autobiography. Cats run throughout his novels, short stories, letters, essays, travel writing, maxims, and witticisms. And cats run throughout his life story, from his childhood days in Hannibal, Missouri, to his last days at that final home, Stormfield, near Redding, Connecticut. He moved into Stormfield in June 1908, less than two years before his death, and he knew just when it would be

"I simply can't resist a cat, particularly a purring one."
PHOTO COURTESY: THE MARK TWAIN PAPERS, THE BANCROFT LIBRARY, UNIVERSITY OF CALIFORNIA, BERKELEY

fit for occupancy: "I don't want to see it until the cat is purring on the hearth."

When Mark Twain biographers and scholars speak of his closest and most cherished friends, they tend to mention fellow writer William Dean Howells, Reverend Joseph Hopkins Twichell, and Standard Oil director Henry Huttleston Rogers. They typically don't mention Abner, Motley, Stray Kit, Fraulein, Lazy, Buffalo Bill, Soapy Sal, Cleveland, Sin, Satan, Famine, Pestilence, Sour Mash, Appollinaris, Zoroaster, Blatherskite, Babylon, Bones, Belchazar, Genesis, Deuteronomy, Germania, Bambino, Ananda, Annanci, Socrates, Sackcloth, Ashes, Tammany, Sinbad, Danbury, or Billiards. These were just thirty-three of the cats who were certain to capture the attention and win the admiration of the adult Mark Twain. If you counted only thirty-two names, that's because he once had three cats, and since two of them were identical, he used the same name, Sackcloth, for both and luckily both answered to the name. The third, of course, was Ashes.

"I simply can't resist a cat, particularly a purring one," he said. "They are the cleanest, cunningest, and most intelligent things I know, outside of the girl you love, of course." No cats around to be petted, praised, and admired? Mark Twain would have considered it the categorical catalyst for a catastrophe of cataclysmic proportions.

He was by no means anti-dog. To be sure, three of his best-known quotes are wonderfully pro-dog:

- "Heaven goes by favor. If it went by merit, you would stay out and your dog would go in."

- "If you pick up a starving dog and make him prosperous, he will not bite you. This is the principal difference between a dog and a man."
- "The dog is a gentleman; I hope to go to his heaven, not man's."

Still, while dogs ranked heavenly high in his estimation, as you can see, cats were closer to his heart. Mark Twain didn't live at a time when people identified themselves as dog people or cat people. Yet there is no doubt he would have been on the cat side of that equation. In a social-media-driven world, he would have been regularly visiting Facebook to post pictures of himself with a feline friend (there are, in fact, about twenty known photographs of Mark Twain with cats, many of which you'll encounter in this volume). There was something in a cat that stirred not only his affection but his admiration.

"By what right has the dog come to be regarded as a 'noble' animal?" Mark Twain wrote. "The more brutal and cruel and unjust you are to him the more your fawning and adoring slave he becomes; whereas, if you shamefully misuse a cat once she will always maintain a dignified reserve toward you afterward—you will never get her full confidence again."

This was the kind of willful independence Mark Twain understood. He found things to admire about the dog, the donkey, the crow, the elephant, and the bat. He certainly held many animals in high esteem, and he wrote stories attacking cruelty toward animals. He supported anti-vivisection groups, and was proud that his youngest daughter, Jean, founded societies for the protection of animals. Jean inherited that caring nature from her father, who had inherited it from his mother. "Many of the characteristics that made Mark Twain famous were inherited from his mother," Albert Bigelow Paine wrote in his authorized biography of the beloved American writer. "His sense of humor, his prompt, quaintly spoken philosophy, these were distinctly her contribution to his fame." Another contribution was an enormous sympathy for animals. Of Jane Lampton Clemens, Paine wrote, "Her sense of pity was abnormal. She refused to kill even flies."

The "natural ally and friend of the friendless," as her son described her, Jane Clemens once snatched a whip away from a burly cart driver who was beating a horse. She made him promise never to "abuse a horse again." Still, the only animal she permitted as pets were cats. So from the very first, there were cats in Mark Twain's life . . . lots of cats.

"By some subtle sign the homeless, hunted, bedraggled and disreputable cat recognized her at a glance as the born refuge and champion of his sort—and followed her home," Mark Twain wrote in his autobiography. "His instinct was right, he was as welcome as the prodigal son. We had nineteen cats at one time, in 1845. And there wasn't one in the lot that had any character, not one that had any merit, except the cheap and tawdry merit of being unfortunate. They were a vast burden to us all—including my mother—but they were out of luck and that was enough; they had to stay. However, better these than no pets at all; children must have pets and we were not allowed to have caged ones. An imprisoned creature was out of the question—my mother would not have allowed a rat to be restrained of its liberty."

So he was surrounded by cats in childhood, and he was surrounded by cats during the last years of his life. These Stormfield cats, however, he considered far nobler representatives of their species. This was how Paine described the state of feline affairs at Mark Twain's Redding home:

The cat was always "purring on the hearth" at Stormfield—several cats—for Mark Twain's fondness for this clean, intelligent domestic animal remained to the end, one of his happiest characteristics. There were never too many cats at Stormfield, and the "hearth" included the entire house, even the billiard-table. When, as was likely to happen at any time during a game, the kittens Sinbad, or Danbury, or Billiards would decide to hop up and play with the balls, or sit in the pockets and grab at them as they went by, the game simply added this element of chance, and the uninvited player was not disturbed. The cats really owned Stormfield; any one could tell that from their deportment. Mark Twain held the title deeds, but it was Danbury and Sinbad and the others that possessed the premises. They occupied any portion of the house or its furnishings at will, and they never failed to attract attention. Mark Twain might be preoccupied and indifferent to the coming and goings of other members of the household; but no matter what he was doing, let Danbury appear in the offing and he was observed and greeted with due deference, and complimented and made comfortable. Clemens would arise from the table and carry certain choice food out on the terrace to Tammany, and be satisfied with almost no acknowledgement by way of appreciation. One could not imagine any home of Mark Twain where the cats were not supreme.

Between the cat companions of childhood and the cats who reigned supreme at Stormfield, there were cats at the magnificent Hartford, Connecticut, home where the Clemens family lived from 1874 until 1891. There were cats at Quarry Farm, the upstate New York retreat where the family spent many happy summers (overlooking Elmira, New York, this was the

Mark Twain's cats were about the only ones allowed to disrupt a game of billiards.
PHOTO COURTESY: THE MARK TWAIN PAPERS, THE BANCROFT LIBRARY, UNIVERSITY OF CALIFORNIA, BERKELEY

home of his sister-in-law, Susan Crane). There were cats at 21 Fifth Avenue, his Manhattan home from 1904 to 1908. Joe Twichell, the pastor of Hartford's Asylum Hill Congregational Church and one of Mark Twain's dearest friends for forty-two years, observed that he "could scarcely meet a cat on the street without stopping to make its acquaintance."

A reprinted *Harper's Weekly* article that ran under the headline "Mark Twain and the Cat" in the February 23, 1907, edition of the *Seattle Daily Times* began with a reference to a Rudyard Kipling story about "a strange revenge wrought upon an Indian household by one Dana Da, a Hindu of supernatural powers." In the Kipling tale, Dana Da's vengeance took the form of "a visitation of cats." There were, as writer Herman Spencer noted, "cats everywhere . . . cats in the bathroom, cats on the library mantel, cats in the dining-room, cats on the bed, cats under the chair cushions, cats in the victim's boots, cats in his ulster [coat] pockets, cats in his saddle roll, cats sitting on his chest when he awoke in the morning—everywhere, cats." The writer's conclusion: "Mark Twain is the Dana Da of contemporary literature. He has visited us with cats." Spencer remarked on how often cats appear in Mark Twain's writings. He seemed unaware of how cats also were a constant in his life. Yes, everywhere, cats. Mark Twain may have been the Dana Da of literature, but, on the home front, he would have considered Dana Da's curse a blessing. He couldn't get enough of cats, and they were allowed to be everywhere.

"Mark Twain had a special fondness for cats," Paine wrote. "As a boy he always owned one and it generally had a seat beside him at the table. There were cats at Quarry Farm and at Hartford, and in the house at Redding. . . . Kittens capering about were his chief delight." Perhaps one reason Bermuda remained a favorite destination was that it had, in his words, "upwards of a million cats."

Mark Twain also used cats in a figurative sense to make a point. Writing to Howells in 1904, he called an "autobiography the truest of all books," even though "the author-cat is raking dust upon it which hides from disinterested spectator neither it nor its smell—the result being that the reader knows the author in spite of his wily diligences." Discussing his brother Orion's ever-changing political and religious beliefs, Mark Twain said he never "acquired a conviction that could survive a disapproving remark from a cat." In *The Innocents Abroad,* he says "a man hauls on a kid glove like he was dragging a cat out of an ash-hole by the tail." In *The Innocents Abroad,* he remarks that a French guide "stepped as gently and as daintily as a cat crossing a muddy street." Describing cramped quarters on a schooner bound for Hawaii, he wrote in *Roughing It* that, "One might swing a cat in it, perhaps, but not a long cat."

Mark Twain compared himself to a cat in an 1895 letter to Rogers, writing that, as a boy, he was nearly drowned nine times in the Mississippi River or Bear Creek "before I learned to swim, and was considered to be a cat in disguise."

The family even noticed something cat-like in Mark Twain's bearing, manner, and behavior. "We used to call Father the 'spitting gray kitten' because in many of his spurts of irritation he kept a soft, fuzzy quality in his demeanor that reminded us of a little kitten with its fur all ruffled," his daughter Clara wrote in her 1931 book, *My Father Mark Twain.* "We enjoyed this spectacle, and were inclined to inspire it whenever we could. When his performance was ended, we would exclaim, 'Oh, you bad, spitting gray kitten!' and he would laugh a gay little laugh and shake his leonine head of gray curls."

He was delighted that Susy and Clara shared his great affection for cats. In a letter written to Twichell from Quarry Farm in late August 1880, he recorded the girls' enthusiasm for their month-old sister, Jean. "Four weeks ago the children still put Mamma at the head of the list" of their favorites, he wrote, but now the order is Jean first, followed by Mamma, Motley, Fraulein, and, in fifth place, Papa. "Some time ago it used to be nip & tuck between me & the cats," Mark Twain observed, "but after the cats 'developed' I didn't stand any more show."

Clara also recalled that if you were going to interrupt her father while he working, it was "expedient to be accompanied by a kitten." Such was the great charm cats had for him. "Never could have too many cats to suit him," remembered longtime family servant Katy Leary, "which is a good sign in a man."

As both Geismar and Fishkin note, the animal Mark Twain regarded with the most doubt and suspicion was the human kind. "Such is the human race," he wrote near the end of his life. "Often it does seem such a pity that Noah and his party did not miss the boat." Yet there was one way a human being ("The Lowest Animal") could earn the benefit of the doubt with him: "When a man loves cats, I am his friend and comrade, without further introduction."

He may have had his doubts about human beings, but, as you will see, never about cats. What follows, then, is a cat-centric trip through Mark Twain's life and literary works.

Anecdotes and maxims are mixed with selections from his correspondence and various books—all arranged to move as nimbly as one of those cats he so admired. As the man said, if you love cats, you're already his friend and comrade, without further introduction. So, without further introduction, please enjoy your time in the company of Mark Twain and his cats.

A March 1883 *Life* magazine sketch of Mark Twain.

PART I

CATS WHO EAT COCOANUTS, SMOKE CIGARS, AND GET BLOWN UP

A cat is more intelligent than people believe,

and can be taught any crime.

—MARK TWAIN, *1894 notebook entry*

1.

THE CAT WHO SWALLOWED THE PAINKILLER
(from *The Adventures of Tom Sawyer*)

———————

Chapter 12 of The Adventures of Tom Sawyer, *published in 1875, finds Tom despondent because his beloved Becky Thatcher is sick and because Muff Potter has been arrested for a murder he and Huck Finn know Injun Joe committed. Aunt Polly believes she knows what will cure his ailments. Mark Twain modeled Aunt Polly on his mother, Jane Lampton Clemens. He was told, "I was a sickly and precarious and tiresome and uncertain child and lived mainly on allopathic medicines during the first seven years of my life." As a result, he recalled in a 1901 speech, he continued to be the family's primary consumer of patent medicines: "I was the subject of my mother's experiment. She was wise. She made experiments cautiously. She didn't pick out just any child in the flock. No, she chose judiciously. She chose one she could spare . . . so I had to take all of the experiments." He remembered one "medicine called Patterson's Patent Pain Killer," which went down "like liquid fire and fairly doubled us up." All of these memories fueled the fiery pain killer in this chapter drawn from Mark Twain's boyhood days.*

———————••—•—•••———————

One of the reasons why Tom's mind had drifted away from its secret troubles was, that it had found a new and weighty matter to interest itself about. Becky Thatcher had stopped coming to school. Tom had struggled with his pride a few days, and tried to "whistle her down the wind," but failed. He began to find himself hanging around her father's house, nights, and feeling very miserable. She was ill. What if she should die! There was distraction in the thought. He no longer took an interest in war, nor even in piracy. The charm of

Peter the cat as depicted in a sketch by True Williams for the first edition of *The Adventures of Tom Sawyer*.

life was gone; there was nothing but dreariness left. He put his hoop away, and his bat; there was no joy in them any more. His aunt was concerned. She began to try all manner of remedies on him. She was one of those people who are infatuated with patent medicines and all newfangled methods of producing health or mending it. She was an inveterate experimenter in these things. When something fresh in this line came out she was in a fever, right away, to try it; not on herself, for she was never ailing, but on anybody else that came handy. She was a subscriber for all the "Health" periodicals and phrenological frauds; and the solemn ignorance they were inflated with was breath to her nostrils. All the "rot" they contained about ventilation, and how to go to bed, and how to get up, and what to eat, and what to drink, and how much exercise to take, and what frame of mind to keep one's self in, and what sort of clothing to wear, was all gospel to her, and she never observed that her health journals of the current month customarily upset everything they had recommended the month before. She was as simple-hearted and honest as the day was long, and so she was an easy victim. She gathered together her quack periodicals and her quack medicines, and thus armed with death, went about on her pale horse, metaphorically speaking, with "hell following after." But she never suspected that she was not an angel of healing and the balm of Gilead in disguise, to the suffering neighbors.

The water treatment was new, now, and Tom's low condition was a windfall to her. She had him out at day-light every morning, stood him up in the woodshed and drowned him with a deluge of cold water; then she scrubbed him down with a towel like a file, and so brought him to; then she rolled him up in a wet sheet and put him away under blankets till she sweated his soul clean and "the yellow stains of it came through his pores"—as Tom said.

Yet notwithstanding all this, the boy grew more and more melancholy and pale and dejected. She added hot baths, sitz baths, shower baths, and plunges. The boy remained as dismal as a hearse. She began to assist the water with a slim oatmeal diet and blister plasters. She calculated his capacity as she would a jug's, and filled him up every day with quack cure-alls.

Tom had become indifferent to persecution by this time. This phase filled the old lady's heart with consternation. This indifference must be broken up at any cost. Now she heard of Painkiller for the first time. She ordered a lot at once. She tasted it and was filled with gratitude. It was simply fire in a liquid form. She dropped the water treatment and everything else, and pinned her faith to Painkiller. She gave Tom a teaspoonful and watched with the deepest anxiety for the result. Her troubles were instantly at rest, her soul at peace again; for the "indifference" was broken up. The boy could not have shown a wilder, heartier interest, if she had built a fire under him.

Tom felt that it was time to wake up; this sort of life might be romantic enough, in his blighted condition, but it was getting to have too little sentiment and too much distracting variety about it. So he thought over various plans for relief, and finally hit upon that of professing to be fond of Painkiller. He asked for it so often that he became a nuisance, and his aunt ended by telling him to help himself and quit bothering her. If it had been Sid, she would have had no misgivings to alloy her delight; but since it was Tom, she watched the bottle clandestinely. She found that the medicine did really diminish, but it did not occur to her that the boy was mending the health of a crack in the sitting room floor with it.

Tom feeding Peter the painkiller, as envisioned by Worth Brehm for a 1910 edition of *The Adventures of Tom Sawyer*.

One day Tom was in the act of dosing the crack when his aunt's yellow cat came along, purring, eyeing the teaspoon avariciously, and begging for a taste. Tom said:

"Don't ask for it unless you want it, Peter."

But Peter signified that he did want it.

"You better make sure."

Peter was sure.

"Now you've asked for it, and I'll give it to you, because there ain't anything mean about me; but if you find you don't like it, you mustn't blame anybody but your own self."

Peter was agreeable. So Tom pried his mouth open and poured down the Painkiller. Peter sprang a couple of yards in the air, and then delivered a war whoop and set off round and round the room, banging against furniture, upsetting flowerpots, and making general havoc. Next he rose on his hind feet and pranced around, in a frenzy of enjoyment, with his head over his shoulder and his voice proclaiming his unappeasable happiness. Then he went tearing around the house again spreading chaos and destruction in his path. Aunt Polly entered in time to see him throw a few double summersets, deliver a final mighty hurrah, and sail through the open window, carrying the rest of the flowerpots with him. The old lady stood petrified with astonishment, peering over her glasses; Tom lay on the floor expiring with laughter.

"Tom, what on earth ails that cat?"

"I don't know, aunt," gasped the boy.

"Why, I never see anything like it. What did make him act so?"

"Deed I don't know, Aunt Polly; cats always act so when they're having a good time."

"They do, do they?" There was something in the tone that made Tom apprehensive.

"Yes'm. That is, I believe they do."

"You do?"

"Yes'm."

The old lady was bending down, Tom watching, with interest emphasized by anxiety. Too late he divined her "drift." The handle of the telltale teaspoon was visible under the bed valance. Aunt Polly took it, held it up. Tom winced, and dropped his eyes. Aunt Polly raised him by the usual handle—his ear—and cracked his head soundly with her thimble.

"Now, sir, what did you want to treat that poor dumb beast so, for?"

"I done it out of pity for him—because he hadn't any aunt."

"Hadn't any aunt! —you numbskull. What has that got to do with it?"

"Heaps. Because if he'd a had one she'd a burnt him out herself! She'd a roasted his bowels out of him 'thout any more feeling than if he was a human!"

Aunt Polly felt a sudden pang of remorse. This was putting the thing in a new light; what was cruelty to a cat might be

The marvelous effects of the painkiller shown in a True Williams illustration for the first edition of *The Adventures of Tom Sawyer*.

cruelty to a boy, too. She began to soften; she felt sorry. Her eyes watered a little, and she put her hand on Tom's head and said gently:

"I was meaning for the best, Tom. And Tom, it did do you good."

Tom looked up in her face with just a perceptible twinkle peeping through his gravity.

"I know you was meaning for the best, Auntie, and so was I with Peter. It done him good, too. I never see him get around so since—"

"Oh, go 'long with you, Tom, before you aggravate me again. And you try and see if you can't be a good boy, for once, and you needn't take any more medicine."

———⋯•⋯———

In April 1908, thirty-three years after the publication of The Adventures of Tom Sawyer, *Mark Twain confirmed in a* New York Times *article headlined "Mark Twain Tells About the Cat" that this chapter was based on an actual childhood incident. "As I was on my way up the hill," he said, "I saw a cat jump over a wall, and that reminded me of a little incident of my childhood. . . . There was a good deal of cholera around the Mississippi Valley in those days, and my mother used to dose up children with a medicine called Patterson's Patent Pain Killer. She had an idea that the cholera was worse than the medicine, but then she had never taken the stuff. . . . I used to feed mine to a crack in the floor of our room when no one was looking.*

"One day when I was doing this our cat, whose name was Peter, came into the room, and I looked at him and wondered if he might not like some of that pain killer. He looked hungry, and it seemed to me that a little of it might do him good. So I just poured out the bottle and put it before him. He did not seem to get the real effect of it at first, but pretty soon I saw him turn and look at me with a queer expression in his eyes, and the next minute he jumped to the window and went through it like a cyclone, taking all the flower pots with him; and seeing that cat on the wall just now reminded me of the little incident of my childhood after many years."

2.

THE CAT WHO WENT OUT ON A LIMB

(Autobiography passage and "Jim Wolf and the Cats" sketch printed in the *New York Sunday Mercury*)

———••———

In his autobiography, Mark Twain recalled the writing of a sketch based on an incident that occurred when he was teenager. Jim Wolf, just a little older than Sam Clemens, worked as a printer's devil, setting type at the Hannibal Journal, *the newspaper run by Orion Clemens, Sam's older brother. He boarded with the Clemens family, and was rendered completely tongue-tied in the presence of Sam's sister, Pamela. One winter's night, Pamela invited several friends to a candy-making party. What happened next is described in this passage from Mark Twain's autobiography, published in the* North American Review *in 1907.*

———••———

I t was back in those far-distant days—1848 or '49—that Jim Wolf came to us. He was from a hamlet thirty or forty miles back in the country, and he brought all his native sweetnesses and gentlenesses and simplicities with him. He was approaching seventeen, a grave and slender lad, trustful, honest, honorable, a creature to love and cling to. And he was incredibly bashful. He was with us a good while, but he could never conquer that peculiarity; he could not be at ease in the presence of any woman, not even in my good and gentle mother's; and as to speaking to any girl, it was wholly impossible. He sat perfectly still, one day—there were ladies chatting in the room—while a wasp up his leg stabbed him cruelly a dozen times; and all the sign he gave was a slight wince for each stab and the tear of torture in his eye. He was too bashful to move.

It is to this kind that untoward things happen. My sister gave a "candy-pull" on a winter's night. I was too young to be of the company, and Jim was too diffident. I was sent up to bed early, and Jim followed of his own motion. His room was in the new part of the house and his window looked out on the roof of the L annex. That roof was six inches deep in snow, and the snow had an ice crust upon it which was as slick as glass. Out of the comb of the roof projected a short chimney, a common resort for sentimental cats on moonlight nights—and this was a moonlight night. Down at the eaves, below the chimney, a canopy of dead vines spread away to some posts, making a cozy shelter, and after an hour or two the rollicking crowd of young ladies and gentlemen grouped themselves in its shade, with their saucers of liquid and piping-hot candy disposed about them on the frozen ground to cool. There was joyous chaffing and joking and laughter—peal upon peal of it.

About this time a couple of old, disreputable tomcats got up on the chimney and started a heated argument about something; also about this time I gave up trying to get to sleep and went visiting to Jim's room. He was awake and fuming about the cats and their intolerable yowling. I asked him, mockingly, why he didn't climb out and drive them away. He was nettled, and said overboldly that for two cents he would.

It was a rash remark and was probably repented of before it was fairly out of his mouth. But it was too late—he was committed. I knew him; and I knew he would rather break his neck than back down, if I egged him on judiciously.

"Oh, of course you would! Who's doubting it?"

It galled him, and he burst out, with sharp irritation, "Maybe you doubt it!"

"I? Oh no! I shouldn't think of such a thing. You are always doing wonderful things, with your mouth."

He was in a passion now. He snatched on his yarn socks and began to raise the window, saying in a voice quivering with anger:

"You think I dasn't—you do! Think what you blame please. I don't care what you think. I'll show you!"

The window made him rage; it wouldn't stay up.

I said, "Never mind, I'll hold it."

Indeed, I would have done anything to help. I was only a boy and was already in a radiant heaven of anticipation. He climbed carefully out, clung to the window sill until his feet were safely placed, then began to pick his perilous way on all-fours along

Simon Wheeler is depicted with a cat in this 1903 illustration for the Jumping Frog story.

the glassy comb, a foot and a hand on each side of it. I believe I enjoy it now as much as I did then; yet it is nearly fifty years ago. The frosty breeze flapped his short shirt about his lean legs; the crystal roof shone like polished marble in the intense glory of the moon; the unconscious cats sat erect upon the chimney, alertly watching each other, lashing their tails and pouring out their hollow grievances; and slowly and cautiously Jim crept on, flapping as he went, the gay and frolicsome young creatures under the vine canopy unaware, and outraging these solemnities with their misplaced laughter. Every time Jim slipped I had a hope; but always on he crept and disappointed it. At last he was within reaching distance. He paused, raised himself carefully up, measured his distance deliberately, then made a frantic grab at the nearest cat—and missed it. Of course he lost his balance. His heels flew up, he struck on his back, and like a rocket he darted down the roof feet first, crashed through the dead vines, and landed in a sitting position in fourteen saucers of red-hot candy, in the midst of all that party—and dressed as he was—this lad who could not look a girl in the face with his clothes on. There was a wild scramble and a storm of shrieks, and Jim fled up the stairs, dripping broken crockery all the way.

The incident was ended. But I was not done with it yet, though I supposed I was. Eighteen or twenty years later I arrived in New York from California, and by that time I had failed in all my other undertakings and had stumbled into literature without intending it. This was early in 1867. I was offered a large sum to write something for the *Sunday Mercury*, and I answered with the tale of "Jim Wolf and the Cats." I also collected the money for it—twenty-five dollars. It seemed over-pay, but I did not say anything about that, for I was not so scrupulous then as I am now.

———————————

This is the sketch as it appeared in the July 14, 1867, edition of the New York Sunday Mercury. Mark Twain uses a fictional narrator, Simon Wheeler, changing Pamela's name to Mary, but using Jim's real name. He also used Simon Wheeler to tell the "Jumping Frog" story. Wheeler's narrative for "Jim Wolf and the Cats" was written in dialect, a popular device for humorists at that time, and the sketch shows how Mark Twain transformed a Hannibal memory into humorous piece for a growing audience.

I knew by the sympathetic glow upon his bald head—I knew by the thoughtful look upon his face—I knew by the emotional flush upon the strawberry on the end of the old liver's nose, that Simon Wheeler's memory was busy with the olden time. And so I prepared to leave, because all these were symptoms of a reminiscence—signs that he was going to be delivered of another of his tiresome personal experiences—but I was too slow; he got the start of me. As nearly as I can recollect, the infliction was couched in the following language:

"We was all boys, then, and didn't care for nothing, and didn't have no troubles, and didn't worry about nothing only how to shirk school and keep up a revivin' state of devilment all the time. Thish-yar Jim Wolf I was a talking about, was the 'prentice, and he was the best-hearted feller, he was, and the most forgivin' and onselfish I ever see—well, there couldn't be a more bullier boy than what he was, take him how you would; and sorry enough I was when I see him for the last time.

"Me and Henry was always pestering him and plastering hoss-bills on his back and putting bumble-bees in his bed, and so on, and some times we'd crowd in and bunk with him, not'thstanding his growling, and then we'd let on to get mad and fight acrost him, so as to keep him stirred up like. He was nineteen, he was, and long, and lank, and bashful, and we was fifteen and sixteen, and tolerable lazy and worthless.

"So, that night, you know, that my sister Mary give the candy-pullin', they started us off to bed early, so as the comp'ny could have full swing, and we rung in on Jim to have some fun.

"Our winder looked out onto the roof of the ell, and about ten o'clock a couple of old tom-cats got to rairin' and chargin' around on it and carryin' on like sin. There was four inches of snow on the roof, and it was froze so that there was a right smart crust of ice on it, and the moon was shining bright, and we could see them cats like daylight. First, they'd stand off and e-yow-yow-yow, just the same as if they was a cussin' one another, you know, and bow up their backs and bush up their tails, and swell around and spit, and then all of a sudden the gray cat he'd snatch a handful of fur out of the yaller cat's ham, and spin him eround, like the button on a barn-door. But the yaller cat was game, and he'd come and clinch, and the way they'd gouge, and bite, and howl; and the way they'd make the fur fly was powerful.

"Well, Jim, he got disgusted with the row, and 'lowed he'd climb out there and snake him off'n that roof. He hadn't reely no notion of doin' it, likely, but we everlastin'ly dogged him and bullyragged him, and 'lowed he'd always bragged how he wouldn't take a dare, and so on, till bimeby he highsted up the winder, and lo and behold you, he went—went exactly as he was—nothin' on but a shirt, and it was short. But you ought to a seen him! You ought to seen him cre-e-epin' over that ice, and diggin' his toe nails and his finger-nails in for to keep from slippin'; and 'bove all, you ought to seen that shirt a flappin' in the wind, and them long, ridicklous shanks of his'n a-glistenin' in the moonlight.

"Them comp'ny folks was down there under the eaves, the whole squad of 'em under that ornery shed of old dead Washn'ton Bower vines—all sett'n round about two dozen sassers of hot candy, which they'd sot in the snow to cool. And they was laughin' and talkin' lively; but bless you, they didn't know nothin' 'bout the panorama that was goin' on over their heads. Well, Jim, he went a-sne-akin' and a sneakin' up, onbe-knowns to them tom-cats—they was a swishin' their tails and yow-yowin' and threatenin' to clinch, you know, and not payin' any attention—he went a-sne-eakin' and a-sne-eakin' right up to the comb of the roof, till he was, in a foot 'n' a half of 'em, and then all of a sudden he made a grab for the yaller cat! But by Gosh he missed fire and slipped his holt, and his heels flew up and he flopped on his back and shot off'n that roof like a dart!—went a smashin' and a-crashin' down through them old rusty vines and landed right in the dead centre of all them comp'ny-people!—sot down like a yearth-quake in them two dozen sassers of red-hot candy, and let off a howl that was hark f'm the tomb! Them girls—well they left, you know. They see he warn't dressed for comp'ny, and so they left. All done in a second, it was just one little war whoop and a whish! of their dresses, and blame the wench of 'em was in sight anywhers!

"Jim, he was a sight. He was gormed with that bilin' hot molasses candy clean down to his heels, and had more busted sassers hangin' to him than if he was a Injun princess—and he came a prancin' up-stairs just a-whoopin' and a cussin', and every jump he give he shed some china, and every squirm he fetched he dripped some candy!

"And blistered! Why bless your soul, that pore cretur couldn't reely set down comfortable for as much as four weeks."

———————

The story of this sketch does not end here. Let us return to the autobiography for more on "Jim Wolf and the Cats."

———————

A year or two later "Jim Wolf and the Cats" appeared in a Tennessee paper in a new dress—as to spelling; it was masquerading in a Southern dialect. The appropriator of the tale had a wide reputation in the West and was exceedingly popular. Deservedly so, I think. He wrote some of the breeziest and funniest things I have ever read, and did his work with distinguished ease and fluency. His name has passed out of my memory.

A couple of years went by; then the original story cropped up again and went floating around in the original spelling, and with my name to it. Soon, first one paper and then another fell upon me vigorously for "stealing" "Jim Wolf and the Cats" from the Tennessee man. I got a merciless basting, but I did not mind it. It's all in the game. Besides, I had learned, a good while before that, that it is not wise to keep the fires going under a slander unless you can get some large advantage out of keeping it alive. Few slanders can stand the wear of silence.

———————

More than just an early sketch, "Jim Wolf and the Cats" was the first humorous story Sam Clemens ever told. The morning after Jim fell from the roof and retreated upstairs, Sam related the episode to Jimmie McDaniel, a Hannibal friend whose father kept the candy shop. "I thought he would laugh his teeth out," Mark Twain related in his autobiography. "I had never been so proud and happy before and I have seldom been so proud and happy since." So, in a way, cats launched Mark Twain's career as a humorist by launching Jim Wolf off that roof and into Pamela's party. "You did it splendidly," young Sam told Jim when he got back to his room. "Nobody could have done it better; and did you see how those cats got out of there? I never had any idea when you started that you meant to do it that way. And it was such a surprise to the folks down-stairs. How did you ever think of it?"

———————

3.

THE CAT WHO HOWLED
AT A FIDDLE
(from *Life on the Mississippi*)

———••————

Mark Twain's formal education had ended a little before the time he goaded Jim Wolf onto that icy roof in pursuit of those quarreling cats. Wolf also was featured in Mark Twain's earliest known printed sketch, "A Gallant Fireman," an 1851 newspaper piece about an office fire. After working as a journeyman "tramp" printer, Sam Clemens achieved a boyhood dream in 1857 by becoming a cub pilot on the Mississippi River (getting his pilot's license in 1859). Both a cat and a fiddle make an appearance in chapter 14 of Life on the Mississippi, *Mark Twain's 1883 book that contains an account of his days on Mississippi River steamboats.*

———••————

My reference, a moment ago, to the fact that a pilot's peculiar official position placed him out of the reach of criticism or command, brings Stephen W. naturally to my mind. He was a gifted pilot, a good fellow, a tireless talker, and had both wit and humor in him. He had a most irreverent independence, too, and was deliciously easy-going and comfortable in the presence of age, official dignity, and even the most august wealth. He always had work, he never saved a penny, he was a most persuasive borrower, he was in debt to every pilot on the river, and to the majority of the captains. He could throw a sort of splendor around a bit of harum-scarum, devil-may-care piloting, that made it almost fascinating—but not to everybody. He made a trip with good old Captain Y. once, and was "relieved" from duty when the boat got to New Orleans. Somebody expressed surprise at the discharge. Captain Y. shuddered at the mere mention of Stephen. Then his poor, thin old voice piped out something like this:

"Why, bless me! I wouldn't have such a wild creature on my boat for the world—not for the whole world! He swears, he sings, he whistles, he yells—I never saw such an Injun to yell. All times of the night—it never made any difference to him. He would just yell that way, not for anything in particular, but merely on account of a kind of devilish comfort he got out of it. I never could get into a sound sleep but he would fetch me out of bed, all in a cold sweat, with one of those dreadful war-whoops. A queer being—very queer being; no respect for anything or anybody. Sometimes he called me 'Johnny.' And he kept a fiddle and a cat. He played execrably. This seemed to distress the cat, and so the cat would howl. Nobody could sleep where that man—and his family—was.

4.

THE CAT WHO BLOWED UP
(from *Roughing It*)

———••——

"I supposed—and hoped—that I was going to follow the river the rest of my days, and die at the wheel when my mission was ended," Mark Twain wrote. *"But by and by the war came, commerce was suspended, my occupation was gone."* When the Civil War put an end to steamboat trade on the Mississippi River, Sam Clemens joined the Missouri State Guard (not a Confederate outfit, as he would later claim). After two weeks of that, he headed west and tried his hand at silver mining in the Nevada Territory. In February of 1863, working at Virginia City's Territorial Enterprise, he used the pen name Mark Twain for the first time. Moving on to newspapers in San Francisco, he succumbed to the lure of gold mining in 1864. These Western experiences make up the bulk of Roughing It (1872). Two cats are given featured roles in this book. One, Tom Quartz, is introduced in chapter 61, which details Mark Twain's time in the mining camps of Tuolumne, California.

———••——

One of my comrades there—another of those victims of eighteen years of unrequited toil and blighted hopes—was one of the gentlest spirits that ever bore its patient cross in a weary exile: grave and simple Dick Baker, pocket-miner of Dead-Horse Gulch. He was forty-six, gray as a rat, earnest, thoughtful, slenderly educated, slouchily dressed, and clay-soiled, but his heart was finer metal than any gold his shovel ever brought to light—than any, indeed, that ever was mined or minted.

Whenever he was out of luck and a little downhearted, he would fall to mourning over the loss of a wonderful cat he used to own (for where women and children are not, men of kindly impulses take up with pets, for they must love something). And he always spoke of the strange sagacity of that cat with the air of a man who believed in his secret heart that there was something human about it—maybe even supernatural.

I heard him talking about this animal once. He said:

"Gentlemen, I used to have a cat here, by the name of Tom Quartz, which you'd 'a' took an interest in, I reckon—most anybody would. I had him here eight year—and he was the remarkablest cat I ever see. He was a large gray one of the Tom specie, an' he had more hard, natchral sense than any man in this camp—'n' a power of dignity—he wouldn't let the Gov'ner of Californy be

Tom Quartz, the mining cat, in *Roughing It*.

familiar with him. He never ketched a rat in his life—'peared to be above it. He never cared for nothing but mining. He knowed more about mining, that cat did, than any man I ever, ever see. You couldn't tell him noth'n' 'bout placer-diggin's—'n' as for pocket-mining, why he was just born for it. He would dig out after me an' Jim when we went over the hills prospect'n', and he would trot along behind us for as much as five mile, if we went so fur. An' he had the best judgment about mining-ground—why you never see anything like it. When we went to work, he'd scatter a glance around, 'n' if he didn't think much of the indications, he would give a look as much as to say, 'Well, I'll have to get you to excuse me,' 'n' without another word he'd hyste his nose into the air 'n' shove for home. But if the ground suited him, he would lay low 'n' keep dark till the first pan was washed, 'n' then he would sidle up 'n' take a look, an' if there was about six or seven grains of gold he was satisfied—he didn't want no better prospect 'n' that—'n' then he would lay down on our coats and snore like a steamboat till we'd struck the pocket, an' then get up 'n' super-intend. He was nearly lightnin' on superintending.

"Well, bye an' bye, up comes this yer quartz excitement. Every body was into it—every body was pick'n' 'n' blast'n' instead of shovelin' dirt on the hillside—every body was put'n' down a shaft instead of scrapin' the surface. Noth'n' would do Jim, but we must tackle the ledges, too, 'n' so we did. We commenced put'n' down a shaft, 'n' Tom Quartz he begin to wonder what in the Dickens it was all about. He hadn't ever seen any mining like that before, 'n' he was all upset, as you may say—he couldn't come to a right understanding of

'bout a mile an' a half into the air.

it no way—it was too many for him. He was down on it, too, you bet you—he was down on it powerful—'n' always appeared to consider it the cussedest foolishness out. But that cat, you know, was always agin new-fangled arrangements—somehow he never could abide 'em. You know how it is with old habits. But by an' by Tom Quartz begin to git sort of reconciled a little, though he never could altogether understand that eternal sinkin' of a shaft an' never pannin' out anything. At last he got to comin' down in the shaft, hisself, to try to cipher it out. An' when he'd git the blues, 'n' feel kind o' scruffy, 'n' aggravated 'n' disgusted—knowin' as he did, that the bills was runnin' up all the time an' we warn't makin' a cent—he would curl up on a gunny-sack in the corner an' go to sleep. Well, one day when the shaft was down about eight foot, the rock got so hard that we had to put in a blast—the first blast 'n' we'd ever done since Tom Quartz was born. An' then we lit the fuse 'n' clumb out 'n' got off 'bout fifty yards—'n' forgot 'n' left Tom Quartz sound asleep on the gunny-sack. In 'bout a minute we seen a puff of smoke bust up out of the hole, 'n' then everything let go with an awful crash, 'n' about four million ton of rocks 'n' dirt 'n' smoke 'n' splinters shot up 'bout a mile an' a half into the air, an' by George, right in the dead center of it was old Tom Quartz a-goin' end over end, an' a-snortin' an' a-sneez'n', an' a-clawin' an' a-reachin' for things like all possessed. But it warn't no use, you know, it warn't no use. An' that was the last we see of him for about two minutes 'n' a half, an' then all of a sudden it begin to rain rocks and rubbage, an' directly he come down ker-whop about ten foot off f'm where we stood. Well, I reckon he was p'raps the orneriest-lookin' beast you ever see. One ear was sot back on his neck, 'n' his tail was stove up, 'n' his eye-winkers was swinged off, 'n' he was all blacked up with powder an' smoke, an' all sloppy with mud 'n' slush f'm one end to the other. Well, sir, it warn't no use to try to apologize—we couldn't say a word. He took a sort of a disgusted look at hisself, 'n' then he looked at us—an' it was just exactly the same as if he had said—'Gents, maybe you think it's smart to take advantage of a cat that ain't had no experience of quartz-minin', but I think different'—an' then he turned on his heel 'n' marched off home without ever saying another word.

"That was jest his style. An' maybe you won't believe it, but after that you never see a cat so prejudiced agin quartz-mining as what he was. An' by an' by when he did get to goin' down in the shaft ag'in, you'd 'a' been astonished at his sagacity. The minute we'd tetch off a blast 'n' the fuse'd begin to sizzle, he'd give a look as much as to say, 'Well, I'll have to git you to excuse me,' an' it was surpris'n' the way he'd shin out of that hole 'n' go f'r a tree. Sagacity? It ain't no name for it. 'Twas inspiration!"

I said, "Well, Mr. Baker, his prejudice against quartz-mining was remarkable, considering how he came by it. Couldn't you ever cure him of it?"

"Cure him! No! When Tom Quartz was sot once, he was always sot—and you might 'a' blowed him up as much as three million times 'n' you'd never 'a' broken him of his cussed prejudice agin quartz-mining."

The affection and the pride that lit up Baker's face when he delivered this tribute to the firmness of his humble friend of other days, will always be a vivid memory with me.

At the end of two months we had never "struck" a pocket. We had panned up and down the hillsides till they looked plowed like a field; we could have put in a crop of grain, then, but there would have been no way to get it to market. We got many good "prospects," but when the gold gave out in the pan and we dug down, hoping and longing, we found only emptiness—the pocket that should have been there was as barren as our own. At last we shouldered our pans and shovels and struck out over the hills to try new localities. We prospected around Angel's Camp, in Calaveras County, during three weeks, but had no success.

———••••◆•••———

Mark Twain did find gold of sorts in Angel's Camp, for it was here that he heard that "villainous backwoods sketch," the "Jumping Frog" story, which would become such a sensation. At the end of this chapter of Roughing It, *he offered the following paragraph for those lost by the mining terms used in the story of* Tom Quartz.

————————◆————————

Some of the phrases in the above are mining technicalities, purely, and may be a little obscure to the general reader. In "placer-diggings" the gold is scattered all through the surface dirt; in "pocket"-diggings it is concentrated in one little spot; in "quartz" the gold is in a solid, continuous vein of rock, enclosed between distinct walls of some other kind of stone—and this is the most laborious and expensive of all the different kinds of mining. "Prospecting" is hunting for a "placer"; "indications" are signs of its presence; "panning out" refers to the washing process by which the grains of gold are separated from the dirt; a "prospect" is what one finds in the

first panful of dirt—and its value determines whether it is a good or a bad prospect, and whether it is worth while to tarry there or seek further.

———••——•——••———

Of course, Tom Quartz would have looked with disdain on anyone not knowing all of that.

———••——•——••———

5.

THE CAT WHO ATE COCOANUTS
(from *Roughing It*)

A tall tale by stagecoach passenger George Bemis sets up the other cat encounter in Roughing It, *this one in chapter 7. After recounting some of the whoppers told by Bemis, Mark Twain recalls an encounter with another storyteller known for his grand embellishments and exaggerations.*

I made up my mind that if this man was not a liar he only missed it by the skin of his teeth. This episode reminds me of an incident of my brief sojourn in Siam, years afterward. The European citizens of a town in the neighborhood of Bangkok had a prodigy among them by the name of Eckert, an Englishman—a person famous for the number, ingenuity, and imposing magnitude of his lies. They were always repeating his most celebrated falsehoods, and always trying to "draw him out" before strangers; but they seldom succeeded. Twice he was invited to the house where I was visiting, but nothing could seduce him into a specimen lie. One day a planter named Bascom, an influential man, and a proud and sometimes irascible one, invited me to ride over with him and call on Eckert. As we jogged along, said he:

"Now, do you know where the fault lies? It lies in putting Eckert on his guard. The minute the boys go to pumping at Eckert he knows perfectly well what they are after, and of course he shuts up his shell. Anybody might know he would. But when we get there, we must play him finer than that. Let him shape the conversation to suit himself—let him drop it or change it whenever he wants to. Let him see that nobody is trying to draw him out. Just let him have his own way. He will soon forget himself and begin to grind out lies like a mill. Don't get impatient—just keep quiet, and let me play him. I will make him lie. It does seem to me that the boys must be blind to overlook such an obvious and simple trick as that."

Eckert received us heartily—a pleasant-spoken, gentle-mannered creature. We sat in the veranda an hour, sipping English ale, and talking about the king, and the sacred white elephant, the Sleeping Idol, and all manner of things; and I noticed that my comrade never led the conversation himself or shaped it, but simply followed Eckert's lead, and betrayed no solicitude and no anxiety about anything. The effect was shortly perceptible. Eckert began to grow communicative; he grew more and more at his ease, and more and more talkative and sociable.

Another hour passed in the same way, and then all of a sudden Eckert said:

"Oh, by the way! I came near forgetting. I have got a thing here to astonish you. Such a thing as neither you nor any other man ever heard of—I've got a cat that will eat cocoanut! Common green cocoanut—and not only eat the meat, but drink the milk. It is so—I'll swear to it."

A quick glance from Bascom—a glance that I understood—then: "Why, bless my soul, I never heard of such a thing. Man, it is impossible."

"I knew you would say it. I'll fetch the cat."

He went in the house. Bascom said: "There—what did I tell you? Now, that is the way to handle Eckert. You see, I have petted him along patiently, and put his suspicions to sleep. I am glad we came. You tell the boys about it when you go back. Cat eat a cocoanut—oh, my! Now, that is just his way, exactly—he will tell the absurdest lie, and trust to luck to get out of it again. Cat eat a cocoanut—the innocent fool!"

Eckert approached with his cat, sure enough.

Bascom smiled. Said he: "I'll hold the cat—you bring a cocoanut."

Eckert split one open, and chopped up some pieces. Bascom smuggled a wink to me, and proffered a slice of the fruit to puss. She snatched it, swallowed it ravenously, and asked for more!

We rode our two miles in silence, and wide apart. At least I was silent, though Bascom cuffed his horse and cursed him a good deal, notwithstanding the horse was behaving well enough. When I branched off homeward, Bascom said: "Keep

the horse till morning. And—you need not speak of this—foolishness to the boys."

———————•———————

Mark Twain engaged in a bit of tall-telling himself with this sketch. He never visited Siam, and later newspaper articles maintained that the incident took place in Hawaii. Although only a few paragraphs in the 591-page Roughing It, *"The Cat Who Ate Cocoanuts" made a strong impression, as we see in a story that ran in the November 14, 1915, edition of Florida's* Tampa Tribune. *The story, which gets some of the details of the Mark Twain tale wrong, is datelined Dalton, Georgia.*

———————•———————

Being firmly convinced that it is a direct descendant of the cat made famous by Mark Twain in "Roughing It," a diminutive feline owned by C.S. Carey has acquired an unusual taste for green beans, its appetite being different from Mark Twain's cat in that it craves beans rather than green cocoanuts.

As the readers of "Roughing It" know, the cat was owned by the most monumental liar in the West, and when a delegation of prominent citizens assembled at his home to show him up for a liar in this statement that his cat liked green cocoanut, they saw the cat not only eat the cocoanut but beg for more.

Carey's cat has an unusual fondness for green beans. It has robbed garden after garden, for it likes to pull them off the

The cat eating the cocoanut—a True Williams sketch for the first edition of *Roughing It.*

stalk and devour them. Lately it has grown so lazy that it waits until a distinctive popping announces the fact that a neighbor is stringing beans for dinner.

———————◆———————

The cat that ate cocoanuts still was a handy pop-culture reference when a columnist enlisted her help for a piece titled "Of Cats and Men," which ran in the Springfield Union, *a Massachusetts newspaper, on July 17, 1949.*

The ever-watchful eye of the press looked with admiration this week on a cat named Kiki who arrived in New York from Madrid with his proud mistress. Kiki is unusual in that his favorite drink is not milk but martinis, and he likes baths, taking one every Sunday whether he needs it or not. He answers commands in either Spanish or English, and in other ways has been "educated" as a human, or so says his mistress.

Mark Twain once met a cat in Hawaii who adored fresh coconut, but Kiki seems to have gone the Hawaiian at least one better. Obviously there are uses for such an accomplished animal—the distillers will regard him with warm approval and a new field is opening up in catnip soap and salmon bath salts—but it seems as though Kiki's owner might have missed the point. What we really need is not cats educated like humans, but humans educated like cats.

———•———

Striking an extremely Twainian note, the author of this column uses the arrival of Kiki to make a point that the author of the strong indictments of "humanity" in Letters from the Earth *would have applauded.*

———•———

Match the cats against humans and the latter show up pretty badly. Supposedly endowed with more brains than cats, men have nearly wrecked their world, and besides hunting birds themselves have accumulated a repertory of vices that would cost even a sophisticated European cat at least two lives merely to contemplate. No one ever heard of cats ganging up to fight a war, they don't play practical jokes, beat their women, abuse their children, drive a hundred miles an hour, set houses on fire, stage holdups, rob banks, cheat friends, bear false witness, or any other of the jolly little habits that men seem unable to break.

6.

THE CAT WHO CONQUERED
AN ELEPHANT
(from *The Innocents Abroad*)

———————◆———————

Having made his reputation in the West as a humorist, Mark Twain arrived in New York City in early 1867 and, a few months later, he was part of the Quaker City *excursion that toured Europe and the Holy Land. His account of the journey,* The Innocents Abroad, *became his first best seller. While visiting a zoological garden in France, Twain encountered an animal odd couple we might dub Felix the Cat and Oscar the Elephant. He describes the "strange companionship" in chapter 11 of* The Innocents Abroad, *published in 1869.*

———————◆———————

The boon companion of the colossal elephant was a common cat! This cat had a fashion of climbing up the elephant's hind legs, and roosting on his back. She would sit up there, with her paws curved under her breast, and sleep in the sun half the afternoon. It used to annoy the elephant at first, and he would reach up and take her down, but she would go aft and climb up again. She persisted until she finally conquered the elephant's prejudices, and now they are inseparable friends. The cat plays about her comrade's fore feet or his trunk often, until dogs approach, and then she goes aloft out of danger. The elephant has annihilated several dogs lately, that pressed his companion too closely.

7.

THE CAT WHO SMOKED CIGARS
(letter to the *Alta California*)

———•———

Visiting Hartford, Connecticut, for the first time in January 1868, Mark Twain stayed at the home of John and Isabella Hooker. In a letter to his mother and sister, he wrote, "Puritans are mighty straight-laced, & they don't let me smoke in the parlor, but the Almighty don't make any better people." He wrote more on the smoking ban in an 1868 letter he sent to the San Francisco Alta California.

———•———

At the hospitable mansion where I am a guest, I have to smoke surreptitiously when all are in bed, to save my reputation, and then draw suspicion upon the cat when the family detect the unfamiliar odor. . . . So far, I am safe, but I am sorry to say that the cat has lost caste.

Mark Twain with three things he loved: a white suit, a cigar, and a cat.
PHOTO COURTESY: THE MARK TWAIN HOUSE & MUSEUM, HARTFORD

8.

THE CAT WHO HAUNTED WESTMINSTER ABBEY
(from *Europe and Elsewhere*)

———————◆———————

In "A Memorable Midnight Excursion," an 1872 piece published in the posthumous collection Europe and Elsewhere *(1923), Mark Twain recalled a late-night tour through Westminster Abbey.*

———————◆———————

We were among the tombs; and on every hand dull shapes of men, sitting, standing, or stopping, inspected us curiously out of the darkness—reached out their hands toward us—some appealing, some beckoning, some warning us away. Effigies, they were—statues over the graves; but they looked human and natural in the murky shadows. Now a little half-grown black-and-white cat squeezed herself through the bars of the iron gate and came purring lovingly about us, unawed by the time or the place—unimpressed by the marble pomp that sepulchers a line of mighty dead that ends with a great author of yesterday and began with a sceptered monarch away back in the dawn of history more than twelve hundred years ago. And she followed us about and never left us while we pursued our work.

———————

They are given a tour of the Abbey by the "superintendent of the works—and his daily business keeps him familiar with every nook and corner of the great pile." At one point, the talkative guide shows them Poet's Corner and the graves of David Garrick, Charles Dickens, and old Thomas Parr.

———————

Very old man, indeed, and saw a deal of life. (Come off the grave, Kitty, poor thing; she keeps the rats away from the office, and there's no harm in her—her and her mother.) And here—this is Shakespeare's statue—leaning on his elbow and pointing with his finger . . .

———————

Eventually, their guide leads them to the "little chamberlike chapels, with solemn figures ranged around the sides, lying apparently asleep, in sumptuous marble beds, with their hands placed together."

At one time while I stood looking at a distant part of the pavement, admiring the delicate tracery which the now flooding moonlight was casting upon it through a lofty window, the party moved on and I lost them. The first step I made in the dark, holding my hands before me, as one does under such circumstances, I touched a cold object, and stopped to feel its shape. I made out a thumb, and then delicate fingers. It was the clasped, appealing hands of one of those reposing images—a lady, a queen. I touched the face—by accident, not design—and shuddered inwardly, if not outwardly; and then something rubbed against my leg, and I shuddered outwardly and inwardly both. It was the cat. The friendly creature meant well, but, as the English say, she gave me "such a turn." I took her in my arms for company and wandered among the grim sleepers till I caught the glimmer of the lantern again. Presently, in a little chapel, we were looking at the sarcophagus, let into the wall, which contains the bones of the infant princes who were smothered in the Tower. Behind us was the stately monument of Queen Elizabeth, with her effigy dressed in the royal robes, lying as if at rest. When we turned around, the cat, with stupendous simplicity, was coiled up and sound asleep upon the feet of the Great Queen! Truly this was reaching far toward the millennium when the lion and the lamb shall lie down together. The murderer of Mary and Essex, the conqueror of the Armada, the imperious ruler of a turbulent empire, become a couch, at last, for a tired kitten! It was the most eloquent sermon upon the vanity of human pride and human grandeur that inspired Westminster preached to us that night.

We would have turned puss out of the Abbey, but for the fact that her small body made light of railed gates and she would have come straight back again.

PHOTO COURTESY: THE MARK TWAIN HOUSE & MUSEUM, HARTFORD

PART II

---·•·---

NO HOME COMPLETE
WITHOUT A CAT

There is nothing so valuable in a home as a baby—&
no young home is complete *without* a baby—a baby
& a cat. Some people scorn a cat & think it not an
essential; but the Clemens tribe are not of these.

—MARK TWAIN, *1884 letter*

9.

THE CAT AND
THE BURGLAR ALARM
(from a letter to William Dean Howells)

―――――•――――

*While on that 1867 Quaker City tour, thirty-one-year-old Mark Twain
met seventeen-year-old Charles Langdon. It was in the Bay of Smyrna,
Mark Twain recalled, that young Charley showed him an ivory min-
iature picture of his sister Olivia. Mark Twain maintained it was a
case of love at first sight. She was ten years younger than the former
tramp printer, steamboat pilot, silver prospector, and gold miner. She
was from a wealthy and genteel family in Elmira, New York, and that
family, at first, did not look upon Charley's Quaker City companion as
an ideal match for the fragile Olivia. Less than three years later, however, on February 2, 1870, the wild humorist from the West married
his Livy. They began their married life in Buffalo, but soon moved to
Hartford, Connecticut, the city they would call home for twenty years.
It was here Mark Twain built a fabulous house that biographer Justin
Kaplan described as "part steamboat, part medieval stronghold, and
part cuckoo clock." The splendid house was full of laughter, friends,*

three daughters (Susy, Clara, and Jean), and cats. Livy's pet name for her husband was Youth. And Youth sometimes gave Livy cause to roll her eyes in a bemused way. This is from a June 6, 1880, letter to his close friend, fellow writer William Dean Howells. George Griffin was the Clemens family's butler at their Hartford house. Rosina (Rosa) Hay was governess to the girls.

———————·•·———————

L ast night, when I went to bed, Mrs. Clemens said, "George didn't take the cat down to the cellar—Rosa says he has left it shut up in the conservatory." So I went down to attend to Abner (the cat). About 3 in the morning Mrs. C. woke me and said, "I do believe I hear that cat in the drawing-room—what did you do with him?" I answered up with the confidence of a man who has managed to do the right thing for once, and said "I opened the conservatory doors, took the library off the alarm, and spread everything open, so that there wasn't any obstruction between him and the cellar." Language wasn't capable of conveying this woman's disgust. But the sense of what she said, was, "He couldn't have done any harm in the conservatory—so you must go and make the entire house free to him and the burglars, imagining that he will prefer the coal-bins to the drawing-room. If you had had Mr. Howells to help you, I should have admired but not been astonished, because I should know that together you would be equal to it; but how you managed to contrive such a stately blunder all by yourself, is what I cannot understand."

So, you see, even she knows how to appreciate our gifts.

10.

PAPA IS PARTICULARLY
FOND OF CATS
(from the autobiography)

When Susy Clemens was thirteen, she began writing a biography of her famous father. Mark Twain used excerpts from this manuscript in his autobiography.

We are a very happy family. We consist of Papa, Mamma, Jean, Clara and me. It is papa I am writing about, and I shall have no trouble in not knowing what to say about him, as he is a very striking character.

He is a very good man and a very funny one. He *has* got a temper, but we all of us have in this family. He is the loveliest man I ever saw or ever hope to see—and oh, so absent-minded.

Mark Twain never got over the joy of carrying a cat around on his shoulder, as this picture, taken at his last residence, Stormfield, demonstrates.

He does tell perfectly delightful stories. Clara and I used to sit on each arm of his chair and listen while he told us stories about the pictures on the wall.

———••••••———

Susy's spelling was sometimes suspect, but Mark Twain made sure not to "profane" her account by correcting it. "The spelling is frequently desperate," he said, "but it was Susy's, and it shall stand."

———••••••———

He is very fond of animals particularly of cats, we had a dear little grey kitten once, that he named "Lazy" (papa always wears grey to match his hair and eyes) and he would carry him around on his shoulder, it was a mighty pretty sight! the grey cat sound asleep against papa's grey coat and hair. The names that he has given our different cats, are realy remarkably funny, they are namely "Stray Kit," "Abner," "Motly," "Freulein," "Lazy," "Buffalo Bill" and "Soapy Sal," "Cleveland," "Sour Mash" and "Famine."

11.

THE CAT IN THE RUFF
(from the autobiography)

———————

With Mark Twain for a father, Susy, Clara, and Jean Clemens had an in-house storyteller. And he was expected to not only furnish stories, but original ones—and not only original stories, but ones based on objects found in the favorite spot for story time: the Hartford home's warm and cozy library. In this passage from his autobiography, Mark Twain describes the storytelling ritual with his beloved daughters. The cat picture he mentions hung to the right of the library fireplace and depicted a tabby wearing an Elizabethan ruff.

———————

I remember the story-telling days vividly. They were a difficult and exacting audience—those little creatures.

Along one side of the library in the Hartford home, the bookshelves joined the mantelpiece—in fact, there were

The magnificent chimneypiece from Ayton Castle in Scotland was the focus for stories told by Mark Twain to his daughters in the first-floor library of their Hartford home (the Cat in the Ruff picture that started many stories is at the right).
PHOTO COURTESY: LIBRARY OF CONGRESS, PRINTS AND PHOTOGRAPHS

shelves on both sides of the mantelpiece. On these shelves and on the mantelpiece stood various ornaments. At one end of the procession was a framed oil painting of a cat's head; at the other end was a head of a beautiful young girl, life size—called Emmeline, because she looked just about like that—an impressionist water-color. Between the one picture and the other were twelve or fifteen of the bric-a-brac things already mentioned, also an oil painting by Elihu Vedder, "The Young Medusa." Every now and then the children required me to construct a romance—and into that romance I had to get all that bric-a-brac and the three pictures. I had to start always

The Cat in the Ruff
PHOTO COURTESY: THE MARK TWAIN HOUSE & MUSEUM,
HARTFORD

with the cat and finish with Emmeline. I was never allowed the refreshment of a change, end for end. It was not permissible to introduce a bric-a-brac ornament into the story out of its place in the procession.

These bric-a-bracs were never allowed a peaceful day, a reposeful day, a restful Sabbath. In their lives there was no peace. They knew no existence but a monotonous career of violence and bloodshed. In the course of time the bric-a-brac and the pictures showed wear. It was because they had had so many and such violent adventures in their romantic careers.

As romancer to the children I had a hard time, even from the beginning. If they brought me a picture, in a magazine, and required me to build a story to it, they would cover the rest of the page with their pudgy hands to keep me from stealing an idea from it. The stories had to come hot from the bat, always.

They had to be absolutely original and fresh. Sometimes the children furnished me simply a character or two, or a dozen, and required me to start out at once on that slim basis and deliver those characters up to a vigorous and entertaining life of crime. If they heard of a new trade, or an unfamiliar animal, or anything like that, I was pretty sure to have to deal with those things in the next romance. Once Clara required me to build a sudden tale out of a plumber and a "bawgunstrictor," and I had to do it. She didn't know what a boa-constrictor was, until he developed in the tale—then she was better satisfied with it than ever.

12.

"A CAT-TALE"
(from *Letters from the Earth*)

———————

The nightly story inspired this humorous piece from Mark Twain, not published until Frederick Anderson featured it in a small, limited-run 1959 book, Concerning Cats: Two Tales by Mark Twain. *Three years later, it reached a much wider audience with the publication of* Letters from the Earth *(edited by Bernard DeVoto). The whimsical tale includes two original cat drawings by Mark Twain and begins with an italicized explanatory note from him.*

———————

My little girls—Susy, aged eight, and Clara, six—often require me to help them get to sleep, nights, by telling them original tales. They think my tales are better than paregoric, and quicker. While I talk, they make comments and ask questions, and we have a pretty good time. I thought maybe other little people might like to try one of my narcotics—so I offer this one.

—M.T.

O nce there was a big noble cat, whose Christian name was Catasauqua—because she lived in that region—but she did not have any surname, because she was a short-tailed cat—being a Manx—and did not need one. It is very just and becoming in a long-tailed cat to have a surname, but it would be very ostentatious, and even dishonorable, in a Manx. Well, Catasauqua had a beautiful family of catlings; and they were of different colors, to harmonize with their characters. Cattaraugus, the eldest, was white, and he had high impulses and a pure heart; Catiline, the youngest, was black, and he had a self-seeking nature, his motives were nearly always base, he was truculent and insincere. He was vain and foolish, and often said he would rather be what he was, and live like a bandit, yet have none above him, than be a cat-o'-nine-tails and eat with the King. He hated his harmless and unoffending little cater-cousins, and frequently drove them from his presence with imprecations, and at times even resorted to violence.

SUSY: What are catercousins, Papa?

Quarter-cousins—it so set down in the big dictionary. You observe I refer to it every now and then. This is because I do not wish to make any mistakes, my purpose being to instruct as well as entertain. Whenever I use a word which you do not understand, speak up and I will look and find out what it means. But do not interrupt me except for cause, for I am always excited when I am erecting history, and want to get on. Well, one day Catasauqua met with a misfortune; her house burned down. It was the very day after it had been insured for double its value, too—how singular! Yes, and how lucky! This often happens. It teaches us that mere loading a house down with insurance isn't going to save it. Very well, Catasauqua took the insurance money and built a new house; and a much better one, too; and what is more, she had money left to add a gaudy concatenation of extra improvements with. Oh, I tell you! What she didn't know about catallactics no other cat need ever try to acquire.

CLARA: What is catallactics, Papa?

The dictionary intimates, in a nebulous way, that it is a sort of demi-synonym for the science commonly called political economy.

CLARA: Thank you, Papa.

Yes, behind the house she constructed a splendid large cata-drome, and enclosed it with a caterwaul about nine feet high, and in the center was a spacious grass plot where—

CLARA: What is a catadrome, Papa?

I will look. Ah, it is a race course; I thought it was a ten-pin alley. But no matter; in fact, it is all the better; for cats do not play ten-pins, when they are feeling well, but they *do* run races, you know; and the spacious grass plot was for cat fights, and other free exhibitions; and for ball games—three-cornered cat, and all that sort of thing; a lovely spot, lovely. Yes, indeed; it had a hedge of dainty little catkins around it, and right in the center was a splendid great categorematic in full leaf, and—

SUSY: What is a categorematic, Papa?

I think it's a kind of shade tree, but I'll look. No—I was mistaken; it is a *word*: "a word which is capable of being employed by itself as a term."

SUSY: Thank you, Papa.

Don't mention it. Yes, you see, it wasn't a shade tree; the Catasauqua didn't know that, else she wouldn't have planted it right there in the way; you can't run over a word like that, you know, and not cripple yourself more or less. Now don't forget that definition, it may come handy to you some day—there is no telling—life is full of vicissitudes. Always remember, a categorematic is a word which a cat can use by herself as term; but she mustn't try to use it along with another cat, for that is not the idea. Far from it. We have authority for it, you see—Mr. Webster; and he is dead, too, besides. It would be a noble good thing if his dictionary was, too. But that is too much to expect. Yes; well, Catasauqua filled her house with internal improvements—catcalls in every room, and they are Oh, ever so much handier than bells; and catamounts to mount the stairs with, instead of those troublesome elevators which are always getting out of order; and civet cats in the kitchen, in place of the ordinary sieves, which you can't ever sift anything with, in a satisfactory way; and a couple of tidy ash cats to clean out the stove and keep it in order; and—catenated on the roof—an alert and cultivated polecat to watch the flagpole and keep the banner a-flying. Ah, yes—such was Catasauqua's country residence; and she named it Kamscatka—after her dear native land far away.

CLARA: What is catenated, Papa?

Chained, my child. The polecat was attached by a chain to some object upon the roof contiguous to the flagpole. This was to retain him in his position.

CLARA: Thank you, Papa.

The front garden was a spectacle of sublime and bewildering magnificence. A stately row of flowering catalpas stretched from the front door clear to the gate, wreathed from stem to stern with the delicate tendrils and shining scales of the cat's-foot ivy, whilst ever and anon the enchanted eye wondered from congeries of lordly cattails and kindred catapetalous blooms too deep for utterance, only to encounter the still more entrancing vision of catnip without number and without price, and swoon away in ecstasy unutterable, under the blissful intoxication of its too, too fragrant breath!

BOTH CHILDREN: Oh, how lovely!

You may well say it. Few there be that shall look upon the like again. Yet was not this all; for hither to the north boiled the majestic cataract in unimaginable grandiloquence, and thither to the south sparked the gentle catadupe in serene and incandescent tranquility, whilst far and near the halcyon brooklet flowed between!

BOTH CHILDREN: Oh, how sweet! What is catadupe, Papa?

Small waterfall, my darlings. Such is Webster's belief. All things being in readiness for the housewarming, the widow sent out her invitations, and then proceeded with her usual avocations. For Catasauqua was a widow—sorrow cometh to us all. The husband-cat—Catullus was his name—was no more. He was of a lofty character, brave to rashness, and almost incredibly unselfish. He gave eight of his lives for his country, reserving only one for himself. Yes, the banquet having been ordered, the good Catasauqua tuned up for the customary morning-song, accompanying herself on the catarrh, and her little ones joined in.

These were the words:

> There was a little cat,
> And she caught a little rat,
> Which she dutifully rendered to her mother,
> Who said, "Bake him in a pie,
> For his flavor's rather high—
> Or confer him on the poor, if you'd druther."

Catasauqua sang soprano, Catiline sang tenor, Cattaraugus sang bass. It was exquisite melody; it would make your hair stand straight up.

SUSY: Why, Papa, I didn't know cats could sing.

Oh, can't they, though! Well, these could. Cats are packed full of music—just as full as they can hold; and when they die, people remove it from them and sell it to the fiddle-makers. Oh, yes, indeed. Such is life.

SUSY: Oh, here is a picture! Is it a picture of the music, Papa?

Only the eye of prejudice could doubt it, my child.

SUSY: Did you draw it, Papa?

I am indeed the author of it.

SUSY: How wonderful! What is a picture like this called, Papa?

A work of art, my child. There—do not hold it so close; prop it up on the chair, *three steps away*; now then—that is right; you see how much better and stronger the expression is than when it is close by. It is because some of this picture is drawn in perspective.

CLARA: Did you always know how to draw, Papa?

Yes. I was born so. But of course I could not draw at first as well as I can now. These things require study—and practice. Mere talent is not sufficient. It takes a person a long time to get so he can draw a picture like this.

CLARA: How long did it take you, Papa?

Many years—thirty years, I reckon. Off and on—for I did not devote myself exclusively to art. Still, I have had a great deal of practice. Ah, practice is the great thing! It accomplishes wonders. Before I was twenty-five, I had got so I could draw a cork as well as anybody that ever was. And many a time I have drawn a blank in a lottery. Once I drew a check that wouldn't go; and after the war I tried to draw a pension, but this was too ambitious. However, the most gifted must fail sometimes. Do you observe those things that are sticking up, in this picture? They are not bones, they are paws; it is very hard to express the difference between bones and paws, in a picture.

SUSY: Which is Cattaraugus, Papa?

The little pale one that almost has the end of his mother's tail in his mouth.

SUSY: But, Papa, that tail is not right. You know Catasauqua was a Manx, and had a short one.

It is a just remark, my child; but a long tail was necessary, here to express a certain passion, the passion of joy. Therefore the insertion of a long tail is permissible; it is called a poetic license. You cannot express the passion of joy with a short tail. Nor even extraordinary excitement. You notice that Cattaraugus is brilliantly excited; now nearly all of that verve, spirit *élan*, is owing to his tail; yet if I had been false to art to be true to Nature, you would see there nothing but a poor little stiff and emotionless stump on that cat that would have cast a coldness over the whole scene; yet Cattaraugus was a Manx, like his mother, and had hardly any more tail than a rabbit. Yes, in art, the office of the tail is to express feeling; so, if you wish to portray a cat in repose, you will always succeed better

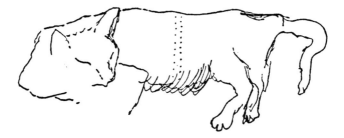

by leaving out the tail. Now here is a striking illustration of the very truth which I am trying to impress upon you. I proposed to draw a cat recumbent and in repose; but just as I had finished the front end of her, she got up and began to gaze passionately at a bird and wriggle her tail in a most expressively wistful way. I had to finish her with that end standing, and the other end lying. It greatly injures the picture. For, you see, it confuses two passions together—the passion of standing up, and the passion of lying down. These are incompatible; and they convey a bad effect to the picture by rendering it unrestful to the eye. In my opinion a cat in a picture ought to be doing one thing or the other, lying down or standing up, but not both. I ought to have laid this one down again, and put a brick or something on her; but I did not think of it at the time. Let us now separate these conflicting passions in this cat, so that you can see each by itself, and the more easily study it. Lay your hand on the picture, to here I have made those dots, and cover the rear half of it from sight—now you observe how reposeful the front end is. Very well; now lay your hand on the front end and cover *it* from sight—do you observe the eager wriggle in that tail? It is a wriggle which only the presence of a bird can inspire.

SUSY: You must know a wonderful deal, Papa.

I have that reputation—in Europe; but here the best minds think I am superficial. However, I am content; I make no defense; my pictures show what I am.

SUSY: Papa, I should think you would take pupils.

No, I have no desire for riches. Honest poverty and a conscience torpid through virtuous inaction are more to me than corner lots and praise.

But to resume. The morning-song being over, Catasauqua told Catiline and Cattaraugus to fetch their little books, and she would teach them how to spell.

BOTH CHILDREN: Why, Papa! Do cats have books?

Yes, catechisms. Just so. Facts are stubborn things. After lesson, Catasauqua gave Catiline and Cattaraugus some rushes, so that they could earn a little circus-money by building cat's cradles, and at the same time amuse themselves and not miss her; then she went to the kitchen and dining room to inspect the preparations for the banquet.

The moment her back was turned, Catiline put down his work and got out his catpipe for a smoke.

SUSY: How naughty!

Thou hast well spoken. It was disobedience; and disobedience is the flagship of the fleet of sin. The gentle Cattaraugus sighed and said, "For shame, Catiline! How often has our dear mother told you not to do that! Ah, how can you thus disregard the commandments of the author of your being!"

SUSY: Why, what beautiful language, for such a little thing, *wasn't* it, Papa?

Ah, yes, indeed. That was the kind of cat he was—cultivated, you see. He had sat at the feet of Rollo's mother; and in the able "Franconia Series" he had not failed to observe how harmoniously gigantic language and a microscopic topic go together. Catiline heard his brother through, and then replied with the contemptuous ejaculation: "S'cat!"

It means the same that Shakespeare means when he says, "Go to." Nevertheless, Catiline's conscience was not at rest. He murmured something about Where was the harm, since his mother would never know? But Cattaraugus said, sweetly but sadly, "Alas, if we but do the right under restraint of authoritative observance, where then is the merit?"

SUSY: How *good* he was!

Monumentally so. The more we contemplate his character, the more sublime it appears. But Catiline, who was coarse and worldly, hated all lofty sentiments, and especially such as were stated in choice and lofty terms; he wished to resent this one, yet compelled himself to hold his peace; but when Cattaraugus said it *over* again, partly to enjoy the sound of it, but mainly for his brother's good, Catiline lost his patience, and said, "Oh, take a walk!"

Yet he still felt badly; for he knew he was doing wrong. He began to pretend he did not know it was against the rule to smoke his catpipe; but Cattaraugus, with an utterance, lifted an accusing paw toward the wall, where, among the illuminated mottoes, hung this one:

"NO SMOKING. STRICTLY PROHIBITED."

Catiline turned pale; and murmuring in a broken voice, "I am undone—forgive me, Brother," laid the fatal catpipe aside and burst into tears.

CLARA: Poor thing! It was cruel, *wasn't* it, Papa?

SUSY: Well but he oughtn't to done so, in the first place. Cattaraugus wasn't to blame.

CLARA: Why, *Susy!* If Catiline didn't *know* he wasn't allowed—

SUSY: Catiline did know it—Cattaraugus told him so; and besides, Catiline—

CLARA: Cattaraugus only told Catiline that if—

SUSY: Why, *Clara!* Catiline didn't *need* for Cattaraugus to say one single—

Oh, hold on! It's all a mistake! Come to look in the dictionary, we are proceeding from false premises. The Unabridged says a catpipe is "a squeaking instrument used in play-houses to condemn plays." So you see it wasn't a pipe to smoke, after all; Catiline *couldn't* smoke it; therefore it follows that he was simply pretending to smoke it, to stir up his brother, that's all.

SUSY: But, Papa, Catiline might as well smoke as stir up his brother.

CLARA: Susy, you don't like Catiline, and so whatever he does, it don't suit you, it ain't right; and he is only a little fellow, anyway.

SUSY: I don't *approve* of Catiline, but I *like* him well enough; I only say—

CLARA: What is approve?

SUSY: Why, it's as if you did something, and I said it was all right. So *I* think he might as well smoke as stir up his brother. Isn't it so, Papa?

Looked at from a strictly mathematical point of view, I don't know, but it *is* a case of six-in-one-and-half-a-dozen-in-the-other. Still, *our* business is mainly with the historical facts; if we only get *them* right, we can leave posterity to take care of the moral aspects of the matter. To resume the thread of the narrative, when Cattaraugus saw that Catiline had not been smoking at all, but had only been making believe, and this too with avowed object of fraternal aggravation, he was deeply hurt; and by his heat was beguiled into a recourse to that bitter weapon, sarcasm, saying, "The Roman Catiline would have betrayed his foe; it was left to the Catasauquian to refine upon the model and betray his friend."

"Oh, a gaudy speech—and very erudite and swell" retorted Catiline, derisively, "but just a *little* catachrestic."

SUSY: What is catachrestic, Papa?

"Farfetched," the dictionary says. The remark stung Cattaraugus to the quick, and he called Catiline a catapult; this infuriated Catiline beyond endurance, and he threw down the gauntlet and called Cattaraugus a catso. No cat will stand that; so at it they went. They spat and clawed and fought until they dimmed away and finally disappeared in a fly fog of cat fur.

CLARA: What is a catso, Papa?

"A base fellow, a rogue, a cheat," says the dictionary. When the weather cleared, Cattaraugus, ever ready to acknowledge a fault, whether committed by himself or another, said, "I was wrong, brother,—forgive me. A cat may err—to err is cattish;

but toward even a foreigner, even a wildcat, a catacaustic remark is in ill taste; how much more so, then, when a brother is the target! Yes, Catiline, I was wrong; I deeply regret the circumstance. Here is my hand—let us forget the dark o'erclouded past in the bright welkin of the present, consecrating ourselves anew to its nobler lessons, and sacrificing ourselves yet again, and forever if need be, to the thrice-armed beacon that binds them in one!"

SUSY: He was a splendid talker, *wasn't* he, Papa? Papa, what is catacaustic?

Well, a catacaustic remark is a bitter, malicious remark—a sort of a—sort of—or a kind of a—well, let's look in the dictionary; that is cheaper. Oh, yes, here it is: "CATACAUSTIC, *n*; a caustic curve formed by reflection of light." Oh, yes, that's it.

SUSY: Well, Papa, what does *that* mean?

13.

SATAN AND SIN
(from the autobiography)

Satan was a cat one of Mark Twain's daughters found on the way to church. The stray was hurried home to their father because they knew of his fondness for cats. Always up for some devilish fun, their father said, "What a nice little cat that is. We'll name him Satan—because he's so black." The deviltry continued when Satan proved fairly conclusively that he was a she, by having a kitten. "How about naming her Sin?" Mark Twain suggested. "She's the daughter of Satan you know." The cats merited a mention in his autobiography.

A t one time when the children were small we had a very black mother-cat named Satan, and Satan had a small black offspring named Sin. Pronouns were a difficulty for the children. Little Clara came in one day, her black eyes snapping with indignation, and said: "Papa, Satan ought to be punished. She is out there at the greenhouse and there she stays and stays, and his kitten is downstairs, crying."

14.

FAST ASLEEP . . . WIDE AWAKE
(from a Mark Twain letter and
a magazine article)

Elmira photographer Elisha M. VanAken visited Quarry Farm during the summer of 1887. When Mark Twain demonstrated his unusual power over the resident cats, VanAken captured the feat with two charming photographs. The story behind the two pictures was recorded by an anonymous writer for a story titled "The Funniest Writer on Earth. Some Anecdotes about Mark Twain," published by The Rambler *on December 24, 1898.*

H e would call [the cats] to "come up" on the chair, and they would all jump up on the seat. He would tell them to "go to sleep," and instantly the group

Fast Asleep

Wide Awake

were all fast asleep, remaining so until he called "Wide awake!" when in a twinkling up would go their ears and wide open their eyes.

———————••—•—••———————

The four cats are Sour Mash, Appollinaris, Zoraoster, and Blath-erskite. Mark Twain wrote in an 1890 letter that the cats' "over-weighted" names were not given to them "in an unfriendly spirit, but merely to practice the children in large and difficult styles of pronunciation. It was a very happy idea. I mean, for the children." The "Fast Asleep" picture was later used as the model for part of a drawing done for Mark Twain's "A Horse's Tale." Mark Twain apparently sent the "Fast Asleep" picture to editor Frederick A. Duneka with an October 1906 letter containing suggestions for illustrations.

———————••—•—••———————

I hope you will reproduce the cat-pile, full page. And save the photo for me in as good condition as possible. When Susy and Clara were little tots those cats had their profoundest worship, and there is no duplicate of this picture. These cats all had thundering names, or inappropriate ones—furnished by the children with my help.

———————••—•—••———————

The illustration in "A Horse's Tale" that used the Fast Asleep picture.

The resulting illustration by Lucius Wolcott Hitchcock was titled, "Look at that pile of cats in your chair." It was used when "A Horse's Tale" ran in two installments in Harper's Magazine *and when the story was published by* Harper's *as a 153-page book in October 1907.*

———••————•———••———

15.

SOUR MASH, SACKCLOTH, AND ASHES
(from the autobiography)

––––––––––––

Of all the cats at Quarry Farm, Mark Twain had a particular fondness for a tortoise-shell he named Sour Mash. Signing off an August 1885 letter to Livy, he wrote, "Kiss the children & Sour Mash for me." The cherished Sour Mash figures in no less than three autobiographical dictations. In the fall of 1906, he spotted a line in Susy's biography of him: "Papa says that if the collera comes here he will take Sour Mash to the mountains." This inspired an extended discussion in praise of Sour Mash, as well as three other cats. The cats he "rented" from a farmer's wife were in Dublin, New Hampshire, where he summered from mid-May to mid-October in 1906.

––––––––––––

This remark about the cat is followed by various entries, covering a month . . . then Susy drops this remark in the wake of the vanished procession:

"Sour Mash is a constant source of anxiety, care, and pleasure to papa."

I did, in truth, think a great deal of that old tortoise-shell harlot; but I haven't a doubt that in order to impress Susy I was pretending agonies of solicitude which I didn't honestly feel. Sour Mash never gave me any real anxiety; she was always able to take care of herself, and she was ostentatiously vain of the fact; vain of it to a degree which often made me ashamed of her, much as I esteemed her.

Many persons would like to have the society of cats during the summer vacation in the country, but they deny themselves this pleasure because they think they must either take the cats along when they return to the city, where they would be a trouble and an encumbrance, or leave them in the country, houseless and homeless. These people have no ingenuity, no invention, no wisdom; or it would occur to them to do as I do: rent cats by the month for the summer and return them to their good homes at the end of it. Early last May I rented a kitten of a farmer's wife, by the month; then I got a discount by taking three. They have been good company for about five months now, and are still kittens—at least they have not grown much, and to all intents and purposes are still kittens, and as full of romping energy and enthusiasm as they were in the beginning. This is remarkable. I am an expert in cats, but I have not seen a kitten keep its kittenhood nearly so long before.

These are beautiful creatures—these triplets. Two of them wear the blackest and shiniest and thickest of sealskin vestments all over their bodies except the lower half of their faces and the terminations of their paws. The black masks reach down below the eyes, therefore when the eyes are closed they are not visible; the rest of the face, and the gloves and

Mark Twain and one of the "rented" kittens on the porch of the Dublin, New Hampshire, house in 1906.
PHOTO COURTESY: THE MARK TWAIN HOUSE & MUSEUM, HARTFORD

stockings, are snow white. These markings are just the same on both cats—so exactly the same that when you call one the other is likely to answer, because they cannot tell each other apart. Since the cats are precisely alike, and can't be told apart by any of us, they do not need two names, so they have but one between them. We call both of them Sackcloth, and we call the gray one Ashes. I believe I have never seen such intelligent cats as these before. They are full of the nicest discriminations. When I read German aloud they weep; you can see the tears run down. It shows what pathos there is in the German tongue. I had not noticed before that all German is pathetic, no matter what the subject is nor how it is treated. It was these humble observers that brought the knowledge to me. I have tried all kinds of German on these cats; romance, poetry, philosophy, theology, market reports; and the result has always been the same—the cats sob, and let the tears run down, which shows that all German is pathetic. French is not a familiar tongue to me, and the pronunciation is difficult, and comes out of me encumbered with a Missouri accent; but the cats like it, and when I make impassioned speeches in that language they sit in a row and put up their paws, palm to palm, and frantically give thanks. Hardly any cats are affected by music, but these are; when I sing they go reverently away, showing how deeply they feel it. Sour Mash never cared for these things. She had many noble qualities, but at bottom she was not refined, and cared little or nothing for theology and the arts.

It is a pity to say it, but these cats are not above the grade of human beings, for I know by certain signs that they are not sincere in their exhibitions of emotion, but exhibit them merely to show off and attract attention—conduct which is distinctly human, yet with a difference: they do not know enough to conceal their desire to show off, but the grown human being does. What is ambition? It is only the desire to be conspicuous. The desire for fame is only the desire to be continuously conspicuous and attract attention and be talked about.

These cats are like human beings in another way: when Ashes began to work his fictitious emotions, and show off, the other members of the firm followed suit, in order to be in the fashion. That is the way with human beings; they are afraid to be outside; whatever the fashion happens to be, they conform to it, whether it be a pleasant fashion or the reverse, they lacking the courage to ignore it and go their own way. All human beings would like to dress in loose and comfortable and highly colored and showy garments, and they had their desire until a century ago, when a king, or some other influential ass, introduced sombre hues and discomfort and ugly designs into masculine clothing. The meek public surrendered to the outrage, and by consequence we are in that odious captivity to-day, and are likely to remain in it for a long time to come.

Fortunately the women were not included in the disaster, and so their graces and their beauty still have the enhancing help of delicate fabrics and varied and beautiful colors. Their clothing makes a great opera audience an enchanting spectacle, a delight to the eye and the spirit, a Garden of Eden for charm and color. The men, clothed in dismal black, are scattered here and there and everywhere over the Garden, like so many charred stumps, and they damage the effect, but cannot annihilate it.

In summer we poor creatures have a respite, and may clothe ourselves in white garments; loose, soft, and in some degree shapely; but in the winter—the sombre winter, the depressing winter, the cheerless winter, when white clothes and bright colors are especially needed to brighten our spirits and lift them up—we all conform to the prevailing insanity, and go about in dreary black, each man doing it because the others do it, and not because he wants to. They are really no sincerer than Sackcloth and Ashes. At bottom the Sackcloths do not care to exhibit their emotions when I am performing before them, they only do it because Ashes started it.

The following year, Mark Twain spent the May-to-October stretch in Tuxedo Park, New York, and he again rented a cat from a neighbor (although he refused to tell a reporter how much he was paying). A week after the autobiographical dictation about Sackcloth and Ashes, Mark Twain again found something in Susy's biography of him that prompted more discussion of Sour Mash. This was what Susy wrote, spelling intact, on September 9, 1885: "Mamma is teaching Jean a little natural history and is making a little collection of insects for her. But mamma does not allow Jean to kill any insects she only collects those insects that are found dead. Mamma has told us all, perticulary Jean, to bring her all the little dead insects that she finds. The other day as we were all sitting at supper Jean broke into the room and ran triumfantly up to Mamma and presented her with a plate full of dead flies. Mamma thanked Jean vary enthusiastically although she with difficulty concealed her amusement. Just then Sour Mash entered the room and Jean believing her hungry asked Mamma for permission to give her the flies. Mamma laughingly consented and the flies almost immediately dissapeared." Mark Twain takes over from here.

———••—•—••———

Sour Mash's presence indicates that this adventure occurred at Quarry Farm. Susy's Biography interests itself pretty exclusively with historical facts; where they happen is not a matter of much concern to her. When other historians refer to the Bunker Hill Monument they know it is not necessary to mention that that monument is in Boston. Susy recognizes that when she mentions Sour Mash it is not necessary to localize her. To Susy, Sour Mash is the Bunker Hill Monument of Quarry Farm.

Ordinary cats have some partiality for living flies, but none for dead ones; but Susy does not trouble herself to apologize for Sour Mash's eccentricities of taste. This Biography was for *us*, and Susy knew that nothing that Sour Mash might do could startle us or need explanation, we being aware that she was not an ordinary cat, but moving upon a plane far above the prejudices and superstitions which are law to common catdom.

———••—•—••———

And then there is this autobiographical dictation from 1906, recalling the Bunker Hill Monument of Quarry Farm (John T. Lewis, a free-born African American who was a tenant farmer at Quarry Farm, was one of the models for Jim in Huckleberry Finn).

━━━━•••━◆━•••━━━

I had a great admiration for Sour Mash, and a great affection for her, too. She was one of the institutions of Quarry Farm for a good many years. She had an abundance of that noble quality which all cats possess, and which neither man nor any other animal possesses in any considerable degree—independence. Also she was affectionate, she was loyal, she was plucky, she was enterprising, she was just to her friends and unjust to her enemies—and she was righteously entitled to the high compliment which so often fell from the lips of John T. Lewis—reluctantly, and as by compulsion, but all the more precious for that:

"Other Christians is always worrying about other people's opinions, but Sour Mash don't give a damn."

Indeed she was just that independent of criticism, and I think it was her supreme grace. In her industries she was remarkable. She was always busy. If she wasn't exterminating grasshoppers she was exterminating snakes—for no snake had any terrors for her. When she wasn't catching mice she was catching birds. She was untiring in her energies. Every waking moment was precious to her; in it she would find something useful to do—and if she ran out of material and couldn't find anything else to do she would have kittens. She always kept us supplied, and her families were of choice quality. She herself was a three-colored tortoise-shell, but she had no prejudices of breed, creed, or caste. She furnished us all kinds, all colors, with that impartiality which was so fine a part of her make. She allowed no dogs on the premises except those that belonged there. Visitors who brought their dogs along always had an opportunity to regret it. She hadn't two plans for receiving a dog guest, but only one. She didn't wait for the formality of an introduction to any dog, but promptly jumped on his back and rode him all over the farm. By my help she would send out cards, next day, and invite that dog to a garden party, but she never got an acceptance. The dog that had enjoyed her hospitalities once was willing to stand pat.

A *New York Herald* sketch of Mark Twain holding a kitten.

16.

UNDERSTANDING CAT LANGUAGE
(from *A Tramp Abroad* and *What Is Man?*)

———————

There are two passages in Mark Twain's writings that will help you understand cat talk. The first is in A Tramp Abroad, and it comes in the form of a tale the writer credits to a California miner named Jim Baker. The story mainly is about a blue jay landing on a roof and finding a hole. Not realizing he's on a roof, he becomes fascinated by how deep the hole is. And tries to fill it with acorns. As his frustration grows, so does the volume of his profanity. But Baker begins his account by comparing the language of blue jays with the language of cats.

———————

There's more *to* a blue-jay than any other creature. He has got more moods, and more different kinds of feelings than other creatures; and, mind you, whatever a blue-jay feels, he can put into language. And no mere commonplace language, either, but rattling, out-and-out book-talk—and bristling with metaphor, too—just bristling! And as for command of language—why *you* never see a blue-jay get stuck for a word. No man ever did. They just boil out of him! And another thing: I've noticed a good deal, and there's no bird, or cow, or anything that uses as good grammar as a bluejay. You may say a cat uses good grammar. Well, a cat does—but you let a cat get excited once; you let a cat get to pulling fur with another cat on a shed, nights, and you'll hear grammar that will give you the lockjaw. Ignorant people think it's the noise which fighting cats make that is so aggravating, but it ain't so; it's the sickening grammar they use. Now I've never heard a jay use bad grammar but very seldom; and when they do, they are as ashamed as a human; they shut right down and leave.

You may call a jay a bird. Well, so he is, in a measure—because he's got feathers on him, and don't belong to no church, perhaps; but otherwise he is just as much a human as you be. And I'll tell you for why. A jay's gifts, and instincts, and feelings, and interests, cover the whole ground. A jay hasn't got any more principle than a Congressman. A jay will lie, a jay will steal, a jay will deceive, a jay will betray; and four times out of five, a jay will go back on his solemnest promise. The sacredness of an obligation is a thing which you can't cram into no bluejay's head. Now, on top of all this, there's another thing; a jay can outswear any gentleman in the mines. You think a cat can swear. Well, a cat can; but you give a bluejay a subject that calls for his reserve-powers, and where is your cat? Don't talk to me—I know too much about this thing. . . .

———••••———

Mark Twain returned to the topic of cat language in What Is Man? *This Socratic dialogue between an Old Man and a Young Man was published anonymously as a book in 1906.*

———••••———

"Dumb" beast suggests an animal that has no thought-machinery, no understanding, no speech, no way of communicating what is in its mind. . . . We understand the cat when she stretches herself out, purring with affection and contentment and lifts up a soft voice and says, "Come, kitties, supper's ready"; we understand her when she goes mourning about and says, "Where can they be? They are lost. Won't you help me hunt for them?" and we understand the disreputable Tom when he challenges at midnight from his shed, "You come over here, you product of immoral commerce, and I'll make your fur fly!"

17.

A FELINE ROYAL FAMILY
(from *A Connecticut Yankee in King Arthur's Court*)

In A Connecticut Yankee in King Arthur's Court, *published in 1889, Mark Twain goes so far as to extol the virtues of a royal family of cats. He put the idea into the mouth of Clarence, the court page who becomes the chief assistant to the Boss, Hank Morgan.*

Clarence was with me as concerned the revolution, but in a modified way. His idea was a republic, without privileged orders but with a hereditary royal family at the head of it instead of an elective chief magistrate. He believed that no nation that had ever known the joy of worshiping a royal family could ever be robbed of it and not fade away and die of melancholy. I urged that kings were dangerous.

He said, then have cats. He was sure that a royal family of cats would answer every purpose. They would be as useful as any other royal family, they would know as much, they would have the same virtues and the same treacheries, the same disposition to get up shindies with other royal cats, they would be laughably vain and absurd and never know it, they would be wholly inexpensive; finally, they would have as sound a divine right as any other royal house, and "Tom VII, or Tom XI, or Tom XIV by the grace of God King," would sound as well as it would when applied to the ordinary royal tomcat with tights on. "And as a rule," said he, in his neat modern English, "the character of these cats would be considerably above the character of the average king, and this would be an immense moral advantage to the nation, for the reason that a nation always models its morals after its monarch's. The worship of royalty being founded in unreason, these graceful and harmless cats would easily become as sacred as any other royalties, and indeed more so, because it would presently be noticed that they hanged nobody, beheaded nobody, imprisoned nobody, inflicted no cruelties or injustices of any sort, and so must be worthy of a deeper love and reverence than the customary human king, and would certainly get it. The eyes of the whole harried world would soon be fixed upon this humane and gentle system, and royal butchers would presently begin to disappear; their subjects would fill the vacancies with catlings from our own royal house; we should become a factory; we should supply the thrones of the world; within forty years all Europe would be governed by cats, and we should furnish the cats. The reign of universal peace would begin then, to end no more forever . . . Me-e-e-yow-ow-ow-ow—fzt—wow!"

Hang him, I supposed he was in earnest, and was beginning to be persuaded by him, until he exploded that cathowl and startled me almost out of my clothes. But he never could be in earnest. He didn't know what it was. He had pictured a distinct and perfectly rational and feasible improvement upon constitutional monarchy, but he was too featherheaded to know it, or care anything about it, either.

18.

HOME IS WHERE THE CAT IS
(from *Pudd'nhead Wilson*)

———————◆———————

This passage from the first chapter of Mark Twain's 1894 novel, Pudd'nhead Wilson, *charmingly sums up his lifelong feelings about what makes for a proper home.*

———————◆———————

When there was room on the ledge outside of the pots and boxes for a cat, the cat was there—in sunny weather—stretched at full length, asleep and blissful, with her furry belly to the sun and a paw curved over her nose. Then that house was complete, and its contentment and peace were made manifest to the world by this symbol, whose testimony is infallible. A home without a cat—and a well-fed, well-petted and properly revered cat—may be a perfect home, perhaps, but how can it prove title?

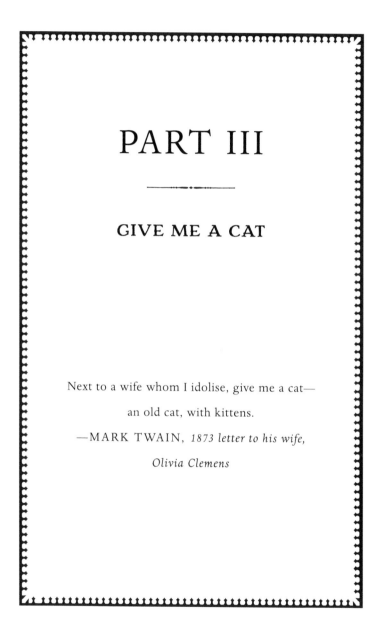

PART III

GIVE ME A CAT

Next to a wife whom I idolise, give me a cat—

an old cat, with kittens.

—MARK TWAIN, *1873 letter to his wife,*

Olivia Clemens

19.

THE CAT AS A LEARNING TOOL
(from *Tom Sawyer Abroad* and *Following the Equator*)

———••——

Mark Twain often extolled the value of experience. "The most permanent lessons in morals are those which come, not of booky teaching but of experience," he wrote in A Tramp Abroad. *"Supposing is good," he said, "but finding out is better." Twice he used a cat to illustrate this point. The first of these can be found in* Tom Sawyer Abroad, *published in 1894.*

———••——

Uncle Abner said that the person that had took a bull by the tail once had learnt sixty or seventy times as much as a person that hadn't, and said a person that started in to carry a cat home by the tail was gitting knowledge that was always going to be useful to him, and warn't ever going to grow dim or doubtful.

Then there's this piece of advice from Following the Equator, *published in 1897.*

We should be careful to get out of an experience only the wisdom that is in it—and stop there; lest we be like the cat that sits down on a hot stove-lid. She will never sit down on a hot stove-lid again—and that is well; but also she will never sit down on a cold one any more.

20.

PRAISE FOR A GERMAN CAT
(from a letter)

———— ••• • ••• ————

Financial woes due to bad investments caused the Clemens family to leave their beloved Hartford home in 1891. They reduced spending a bit by living in Europe. After a stay in Bad Nauheim, Germany, for several months in 1892, they settled in a villa in Florence, Italy. The climate and location suited Mark Twain. There was only one thing he wanted, however, which he mentioned in a letter to Livy's sister, Susan Crane.

———— ••• • ••• ————

What we lack is a cat. If we only had Germania! That was the most satisfactory all-round cat I have seen yet. Totally ungermanic in the raciness of his character and in the sparkle of his mind and the spontaneity of his movements. We shall not look upon his like again . . .

21.

THE KITTENS OF GREAT FALLS, MONTANA
(from memories recorded by James Burton Pond)

———•———

Mark Twain's fortunes fell apart due to disastrous investments, bad business decisions, poor economic conditions, and mismanagement by others. Almost sixty years old and about $100,000 in debt, the ruined writer was determined to crawl his way back to solvency in a manner that would appease both an army of creditors and his own fiery conscience. He heroically resolved to repay all his debts, dollar for dollar. The ninety-six creditors would have settled for less—much less, probably fifty cents on the dollar. Mark Twain would not settle for anything less than complete repayment. The only path open to him was one he had come to loathe—the lecture platform, where he had reigned as America's foremost humorous speaker. He would lecture around the world, then write a travel book about his trip. Beginning in Cleveland on July 15, 1895, he made about 140 appearances on five

Mark Twain admires a little girl's cats at a Great Falls shanty occupied by Norwegian immigrants.
PHOTO COURTESY: THE MARK TWAIN ARCHIVE, ELMIRA COLLEGE, ELMIRA, NEW YORK

continents. Accompanying Mark Twain on his marathon journey were Livy and their middle child, Clara. Traveling with them for the North American leg of the tour was lecture manager James Burton Pond and his wife, Martha. From Cleveland, the tour proceeded to Michigan, Minnesota, and Montana. Booked to lecture at the Opera House in Great Falls, Montana, on July 31, Mark Twain toured the city earlier in the day and happened on a group of shanties occupied by Norwegian immigrants. There were kittens scampering about, and that was certain to arrest his attention. Pond recorded what happened next, both in words and with his Kodak camera.

He caught a pair of kittens in his arms, greatly to the discomfort of their owner, a little girl. He tried to make friends with the child, and buy the kitties, but she began to cry and beg that her pets might be liberated. He soon captured her with a pretty story, and finally consented to let them go.

The next day, the Great Falls Daily Tribune *described Mark Twain's appearance at the Opera House.*

The little girl is won over by the fellow won over by her cats.
PHOTO COURTESY: THE MARK TWAIN ARCHIVE, ELMIRA COLLEGE, ELMIRA, NEW YORK

The inimitable Mark Twain, who has chased away somber thoughts and straightened out the creases in millions of brows by his quaint humor, visited Great Falls for the first time yesterday. . . . The lecture last night was attended by the best people in the city and thoroughly enjoyed by them. It was largely made up from selections from his works. The quaintness and originality of the man and his manner gave an added charm to the stories. The finale of the lecture was a ghost story, which ended with a surprise to the audience, and illustrated as well perhaps as anything the peculiar humor of the man.

22.

A CAT WHO GETS AROUND
(from *Following the Equator*)

Determined to pay off his debts dollar for dollar, Mark Twain embarked on a round-the-world lecture tour in July 1895. The year-long itinerary took him to, among other places, Canada, Hawaii, Australia, New Zealand, India, Ceylon, and South Africa. He poured these experiences into an 1897 travel book, Following the Equator. *Cats make several appearances in this hefty volume. One is on the ship sailing from Sydney to Ceylon.*

Three big cats—very friendly loafers; they wander all over the ship; the white one follows the chief steward around like a dog. There is also a basket of kittens. One of these cats goes ashore, in port, in England, Australia, and India, to see how his various families are getting along, and

A cat knowing when to set sail in *Following the Equator*.

is seen no more till the ship is ready to sail. No one knows how he finds out the sailing date, but no doubt he comes down to the dock every day and takes a look, and when he sees baggage and passengers flocking in, recognizes that it is time to get aboard. This is what the sailors believe. . . .

23.

UNDERMINING THE MORAL FIBER OF A CAT
(from *Following the Equator*)

———————

Chapter 30 of Following the Equator *finds the writer concerned about the endangered morals of the cats of New Zealand.*

———————

I n New Zealand the rabbit plague began at Bluff. The man who introduced the rabbit there was banqueted and lauded; but they would hang him, now, if they could get him. In England the natural enemy of the rabbit is detested and persecuted; in the Bluff region the natural enemy of the rabbit is honored, and his person is sacred. The rabbit's natural enemy in England is the poacher; in Bluff its natural enemy is the stoat, the weasel, the ferret, the cat, and the mongoose. In England any person below the Heir who is caught with a rabbit in his possession must satisfactorily explain how it got there, or he will suffer fine and imprisonment, together with extinction of his peerage; in Bluff, the cat found with a rabbit in its possession does not have to explain—everybody looks the other way; the person caught noticing would suffer fine and imprisonment, with extinction of peerage. This is a sure way to undermine the moral fabric of a cat. Thirty years from now there will not be a moral cat in New Zealand. Some think there is none there now.

24.

A PLACE A CAT
WOULD LIKE
(from *Following the Equator*)

———••————

In chapter 62 of Following the Equator, *Mark Twain describes the westward voyage from Ceylon to the island of Mauritius. The illustration accompanying this passage explains just why a cat would so like that place.*

———••————

L ots of pets on board—birds and things. In these far countries the white people do seem to run remarkably to pets. Our host in Cawnpore had a fine collection of birds—the finest we saw in a private house in India. And in Colombo, Dr. Murray's great compound and commodious bungalow were well populated with domesticated company from the woods: frisky little squirrels; a Ceylon mina walking

A drawing for the first edition of *Following the Equator*.

sociably about the house; a small green parrot that whistled a single urgent note of call without motion of its beak, also chuckled; a monkey in a cage on the back veranda, and some more out in the trees; also a number of beautiful macaws in the trees; and various and sundry birds and animals of breeds not known to me. But no cat. Yet a cat would have liked that place.

25.

BAMBINO

(from memories recorded by
Clara Clemens and Katy Leary)

———••———

After the death of his beloved wife, Livy, in June 1904, Mark Twain settled into a house at 21 Fifth Avenue in New York City. No cat in Mark Twain's life was better documented (or cat-alogued, if you will) than another resident of this Manhattan dwelling, Bambino. In her 1931 book, My Father, Mark Twain, *Clara Clemens recalled how Bambino came to become Mark Twain's cat. Suffering a nervous breakdown after her mother's death, Clara spent about a year recuperating in a Connecticut sanatorium.*

———••———

I n the early autumn Father rented a house on Fifth Avenue, corner of Ninth Street, number 21, where he, Jean, the faithful Katie, and the secretary settled down for the

Photographed by Jean Clemens, Bambino is perched in front of books about birds.
PHOTO COURTESY: THE MARK TWAIN PAPERS, THE BANCROFT LIBRARY, UNIVERSITY OF CALIFORNIA, BERKELEY

winter. I was taken to a sanatorium for a year. During the first months of my cure I was completely cut off from friends and family, with no one to speak to but the doctor and nurse. I must modify this statement, however, for I had smuggled a black kitten into my bedroom, although it was against the rules of the sanatorium to have any animals in the place. I called the cat Bambino and it was permitted to remain with me until the unfortunate day when it entered one of the patient's rooms who hated cats. Bambino came near giving the good lady a cataleptic fit, so I was invited to dispose of my pet after that. I made a present of it to Father, knowing he would love it, and he did. A little later I was allowed to receive a limited number of letters, and Father wrote that Bambino was homesick for me and refused all meat and milk, but contradicted his statement a couple of days later saying: "It has been discovered that the reason your cat declines milk and meat and lets on to live by miraculous intervention is, that he catches mice privately."

———————••■—•—••———————

Katy Leary's memories of her thirty years as a servant with the writer were recorded by Mary Lawton in the 1925 book A Lifetime with Mark Twain.

———————••■—•—••———————

Mr. Clemens borrowed a kitten one time, called Bambino, from Clara, who had him in the sanitarium, and had trained him to wash his own face in the bowl every morning—which shows that he was a very smart little cat. He used to have this kitten up in his room at the Fifth Avenue house and he taught it to put out a light, too. He had a tiny little lamp to light his cigars with at the head of the bed, and after he got all fixed and didn't want the light any more, he taught that cat to put his paw on the light and put it out. Bambino would jump on the bed, look at Mr. Clemens to see if he was through with the light, and when Mr. Clemens would bow twice to him, he'd jump over on to that table quick, and put his little paw right on the lamp! Mr. Clemens was always showing him off; he did that for a lot of people that come there to call.

One night he got kind of gay, when he heard some cats calling from the back fence, so he found a window open and he stole out. We looked high and low but couldn't find him.

A newspaper artist shows Bambino extinguishing the lamp used as a cigar lighter, but the fur should be a solid black.

Mr. Clemens felt so bad that he advertised in all the papers for him. He offered a reward for anybody that would bring the cat back. My goodness! the people that came bringing cats to that house! A perfect stream! They all wanted to see Mr. Clemens, of course.

Two or three nights after, Katherine heard a cat meowing across the street in General Sickles' back yard, and there was Bambino—large as life! So she brought him right home. Mr. Clemens was delighted and then he advertised that his cat was found! But the people kept coming just the same with all kinds of cats for him—anything to get a glimpse of Mr. Clemens!

Bambino did, indeed, go missing in early April 1905, not long after his arrival at 21 Fifth Avenue. Mark Twain offered a reward in the New York American, *and, under headlines like "Mark Twain Has Lost a Black Cat," the notice was reprinted in newspapers all over the country.*

Have you seen a distinguished looking cat that looks as if it might be lost? If you have take it to Mark Twain, for it may be his. The following advertisement was received at the *American* office Saturday night:

A CAT LOST—FIVE DOLLARS REWARD for his restoration to Mark Twain, No. 21 Fifth Avenue. Large and intensely black; thick, velvety fur; has a faint fringe of white hair across his chest; not easy to find in ordinary light.

Bambino's return was heralded as news. Some reports stated he was found in the attic, but Katy Leary insisted he was found in a roomy backyard across the street. Mark Twain told reporters that he couldn't "count high enough" to estimate the number of local black cats anxious to adopt him as their father. With Bambino attracting this much attention, the New York Times *dispatched Zoe Anderson Norris to write a story. After several failed attempts to interview Mark Twain, she decided the best approach was to get the facts from the horse's mouth (or the cat's mouth, in this case). The unsigned article ran April 9, 1905, under the headline "A Talk With Mark Twain's Cat, The Owner Being Invisible."*

Mark Twain had lost his cat. Consumed with an attack of wanderlust, Bambino had fled from home and roamed for a day and a half. The humorist had offered a reward of $5. Then his secretary, Miss Lyon, had met Bambino on University Place and haled him home.

It was all in the papers.

Failing to understand why it shouldn't be in the papers some more, a woman from THE TIMES had called at the Clemens mansion, 21 Fifth Avenue.

A man with china blue eyes and a white waistcoat opened the door for her. He opened it just half way.

Upon her request to see Mr. Clemens, he gave a start of surprise, frowned, and said:

"Mr. Clemens is asleep."

It was then 1:30 in the afternoon.

"When can I see him?" asked the woman.

"I will find out," said the servant, and shut the door upon her while he did so.

By and by he reopened it.

"He may see you," he told her, "if you come back at 5 o'clock."

It was a beautiful sunshiny day, but the woman went home, stayed indoors to rest up for this interview, and at 5 o'clock again sauntered toward the Clemens mansion.

The same man appeared. He wore the same waistcoat. He had, likewise, the same blue eyes.

"Mr. Clemens is not in now," he said, "but his secretary might see you."

"Very well," responded the woman, and stood outside the shut door once more while he searched for the secretary.

As she gazed upon Fifth Avenue, gay in the sunshine with automobiles and carriages and people enjoying themselves, she wondered vaguely if thieves were in the habit of infesting the Clemens mansion; if that was the reason they were so particular about the door.

Then it opened cautiously and the servant said:

"You may come in."

Precious privilege. The woman went in and stood in the hall as if she were a book agent. There were chairs, but she was afraid to sit down.

Presently the secretary, a nice little woman with brown eyes and old-fashioned sleeves, came down the stairs and asked her what she wanted.

"I want to see Mr. Clemens about the cat," replied the woman.

"Mr. Clemens never sees anybody—I mean any newspaper people. Besides, he is not at home."

"Then," said the woman, "may I see the cat?"

"Yes," nodded the secretary, "you may see the cat," and she ran lightly up the long stairway and came down soon with Bambino in her arms, a beautiful black silent cat with long velvety fur and luminous eyes that looked very intelligently into the face of the woman.

The secretary and the woman then sat down on a bench in the hall, and talked about the cat. The cat listened but said nothing.

"We were terribly distressed about him," cooed the secretary. "He is a great pet with Mr. Clemens. He is a year old. It is the first time he has ever run away. He lies curled up on Mr. Clemens's bed all day long."

"Does Mr. Clemens breakfast at five o'clock tea and dine on the following day?" asked the woman.

"Oh, no. He does all his writing before he gets up. That's why he gets up at 5 o'clock. Bambino always stays with him while he writes."

"I should consider it a great privilege," smiled the woman, "to breathe the same atmosphere with Mr. Clemens for about three minutes. Don't you think if I came back at 7 you might arrange it?"

"I will try," promised the secretary, kindly.

At 7, therefore, the woman toiled up the dark red steps and rang the bell. The china-eyed man with the white waistcoat opened the door, disclosed one eye and the half of his face, said abruptly, "Mr. Clemens doesn't wish to see you," and slammed the door.

The woman walked slowly down the red steps and looked up Fifth Avenue, wondering whether she would walk home or take a car.

Fifth Avenue was very beautiful.

Purplish in the dusk, it was gemmed with softly gleaming opalescent electric balls of light.

It was, moreover, admirably bare of people.

She concluded to walk home.

She was about to start forward when she became aware of a furry gentle something rubbing against her skirts.

She looked down, and there was Bambino, purring at her, looking up at her out of his luminous cat eyes.

The man at the door had shut him out, too!

She took him in both hands and lifted him up. He nestled against her shoulder.

"I don't like to prejudice you against the people you have to live with, Bambino," she said. "It seems they will make you live with them. But they weren't so nice. Were they? They might have told me at the start he wouldn't see me. They needn't have made me lose all the sunshine of to-day. You can't bring back a day and you can't bring back sunshine. You wouldn't have treated me like that, would you?"

Bambino purred musically in his earnest assurance that he would not.

"I suppose you heard it all," she went on, "and you sympathized with me. You are awfully tired yourself. I can see that.

If you were a Parisian cat we'd call it ennui, that expresses it better, but we'll let it go at tired. You are. Aren't you? Or you wouldn't have run off."

Bambino sighed wearily and half closed his eyes.

"It's a pretty rarefied atmosphere, I imagine, for a cat," she reasoned. "I don't blame you for wanting to get out with the common cats and whoop it up a little. Any self respecting cat would rather run himself in a gutter or walk the back fence than sit cooped up the livelong day with a humorist. You can't tell me anything about that. It's a deadly thing to see people grind out fun. I used to know a comic artist. I had to sit by and watch him try to match his jokes to pictures!"

She clasped Bambino closer and caught her breath in a sigh.

"I don't blame you one bit for running off," she reiterated. "I can imagine what you must have suffered. Shall we walk along a little on this beautiful street that's so wide and empty now of people?" she asked politely. "I get as tired as you do sometimes of people, Bambino. They are not always so nice. There are a lot of times that I like cats better."

Bambino curled himself up in her arms and laid an affectionate paw on her wrist by way of rewarding her.

She walked on, fondling him.

"I've the greatest notion," she confided presently, "to run off with you and paralyze them. It would serve them right. How would you like, Bambino, to come and live with me in my studio?"

Bambino raised his head and purred loudly against her cheek to show how well he would like it.

"Now, I want to tell you exactly how it will be. I want to be perfectly fair with you. If you come with me you must come with your eyes open. Maybe you won't have half as soft a bed to lie on, but you won't have to lie on it all day long. I'll promise you that. In the first place, it masquerades as a couch full of pillows in the daytime, and in the second place I've got to get out and hustle if I want to eat. Not that I mind hustling. I wouldn't stay in bed all day long out of the sunshine if I could. And you mayn't have as much to eat either, but if you get too hungry there are the goldfish—and the canary wouldn't make half a bad meal. I am pretty fond of both, but I am reckless to-night somehow. You'll be welcome to them."

Bambino licked his chops preparatorily.

"There are a good many little things you are apt to miss. The studio isn't as big as a house by any means, but you'll have all out doors to roam in. I'll trust to your coming home of nights because you'll like it there," she concluded confidently.

"And you'll be rid of the man at the door for good and all. Tell me, now, doesn't he step on your tail and 'sic' the mice on you when they are all away?"

Bambino groaned slightly, but he was otherwise noncommittal.

"I knew he did. He looks capable of anything. He's not as wise as he looks, though. He may not know it, but I push the pen for the tallest newspaper building in the city, the tallest in the world, I think. I'll take you up to the top of that building of mine, and let you climb the flag pole. Then if there should happen to be another cat on the Flatiron Building there'd be some music, wouldn't there, for the rest of the city? And they couldn't throw that flatiron at you anyway, could they? Want to go?"

Bambino put both paws around her neck, and purred an eloquent assent.

"You talk less than anybody I ever interviewed," remarked the woman, "but I think I know what you mean."

She pressed his affectionate black paws against her neck and hurried up the avenue, looking back over her shoulder to see that nobody followed.

She almost ran until she got to the bridge over the yawning chasm near Sixteenth Street. Then she stopped.

Bambino looked anxiously up to see what was the matter.

But she turned deliberately around.

Bambino gave a long-drawn sigh. He looked appealingly up at her out of his luminous eyes.

"I reckon I won't steal you, Bambino," she concluded, sadly. "I'd like to, but it wouldn't be fair.

"In the morning he'd be sorry. Maybe he couldn't work without you there, looking at him out of your beautiful eyes. You don't have to hear him dictate, too, do you Bambino? If I thought that! But no. There is a limit. He's had his troubles, too, you know. He's bound to be a little lenient. The goose hasn't always hung so high for him. Of course you don't remember it, but he had an awful time establishing himself as the great American humorist. Couldn't get a single publisher to believe it. Had to publish his 'Innocents Abroad' himself. Just said to the American public, 'Now, you've got to take this. It's humor,' and made them take it. Held their noses. That was a long time ago. Couldn't do it to-day. Not with 'Innocents

Abroad.' The American public is getting too well educated. Who ever reads 'Innocents Abroad' now? Not the rising generation. You ask any boy of to-day what is the funniest book, and see if he doesn't say 'Alice in Wonderland'?

"Still, for an old back date book, that wasn't half bad. He has never written anything better. It must give him the heartache to see it laid on the shelf. I suppose you must hear these things discussed, but not this side of them, perhaps. No. Naturally no. They don't make you read their books, they can't, but you must have to hear about them. Life is hard! But I must take you back. We mustn't do anything at all to hurt his feelings."

Bambino was fairly limp with disappointment. He had set his heart on the top of The Times Building flagpole. He had almost tasted the canary, to say nothing of the goldfish. He hadn't the heart to purr any longer. He paws fell from the woman's neck. She had to carry him like that, all four feet hanging lifeless, his head drooping.

"And there's another thing, Bambino," she continued, as they went along. "I don't want anything I said about his having to establish himself as a humorist to disillusion you or make you more dissatisfied than you are. All humorists are like that. They have to establish themselves. Why, wasn't I in London when Nat Goodwin produced his 'Cowboy and the Lady' at Daly's? Couldn't I hear people he had planted all over the audience that first night explaining that he was a humorist, and the play was intended to be funny? Certainly. But it didn't work that whirl. Those English people are more determined than we are. They wouldn't stand for it. He had to take the play off.

"Your master happened to catch us when we were young and innocent. He deserves a lot of credit for bamboozling us. You ought to admire him for it. I do."

They were nearly home by now. Bambino managed to emit another purr. It was like a whimper.

"Don't you cry, Bambino," she soothed. "We all have our troubles. You must be a brave cat and bear up under yours," and she tiptoed up the red steps and set him at the door where they could find him when they missed him.

He sat there, a crumpled, black, discouraged ball, his eyes following her hungrily.

She ran back to him.

"Bear up under it the best you can, Bambino," she implored; "but if it gets so you can't stand it again, you know where to find a friend."

There was a sound of approaching footsteps in the hall.

She pressed her lips to Bambino's ear, whispered her address to him, and fled.

Born February 29, 1860, in Kentucky, writer and social worker Zoe Anderson Norris contributed stories to newspapers and magazines until her death in February 1914. Although the story ran without a byline, she wrote about the "interview" and its aftermath in a December 1906 article published in The Bohemian *("A Clever Magazine for Clever People"). It was reprinted in several newspapers.*

I was working for a certain New York paper. I had made a great hit up there with an interview with Mrs. Reader, the promoter, so great a hit that everybody in the Sunday department arose when I entered the room and offered me chairs, and my wages were raised!

"I see," said the Sunday editor, "that Mark Twain's cat has run away. Go down and find out why. Get an interview with Mr. Clemens if you can, and bring it to me."

I forthwith meandered down and hung about the beautiful Fifth avenue residence of the noted humorist for the length and breadth of a sunny afternoon. He would see me after luncheon, said the blue-eyed butler first—he had eyes like a china doll's. Then he would see me at 5 o'clock tea; he seldom got up till 5, the butler informed me, and the cat lay curled up by him through the day. And then at 5 o'clock the butler told me he would see me at dinner time. At dinner time the blue-eyed butler slammed the distinguished door in my common-or-garden face with a curt: "Mr. Clemens doesn't care to see you at all."

Well! The cat had got out of the bed of the humorist, and coming down to see what the matter was, had been shut out, too. He brushed against my desolate skirts as I went down the steps, grieving over my lost afternoon and opportunity. I took him up in my arms, and, walking down the street with him, interviewed him. I condoled with him for being obliged to lie curled up all day long on the bed of the alleged humorist—yes, that is what I dared to call him in my chagrin. I told him I didn't blame him at all for running away, I would have done the same exactly, and added a few more caustic remarks on the same order and in the same vein.

The interview with the cat was published.

On the following Monday I went cheerily to the office for my weekly suggestions as to work. I was met by a frigid silence, the thickness of ice. They raised their heads and looked me over, but almost immediately lowered them again. Not a soul of them arose, as ordinarily, to offer me a chair. But I was permitted to stand there against the door without being ordered out, and that was something.

It was not long before I discovered the why and wherefore. I had offended a great man, the leading humorist of the day. I had dared to have some fun out of him. As a matter of fact, I understood later that he had laughed at the article, but then they didn't know that. A thundering reprimand had come down from the office of the proprietor. The Sunday editor, on account of that interview of mine with Mark Twain's cat, had come within an ace of losing his job.

It required some weeks of tactful diplomacy to reinstate myself with the Sunday editor, but after that I took the precaution to carry a little campstool along with me to that office, so as to be sure of a place to sit down should I possess the inclination.—From "A Common or Garden Reporter"

Bambino also was recalled by Colonel George Harvey, Mark Twain's publisher, in a March 1905 article published in the Washington Post.

I think that perhaps the funniest thing about Mark Twain now is not his writing, but his bed. He lies in bed a good deal; he says he has formed the habit. His bed is the largest one I ever saw, and on it is the weirdest collection of objects you ever saw, enough to furnish a Harlem flat—books, writing materials, clothes, any and everything that could foregather in his vicinity.

He looks quite happy rising out of the mass, and over all prowls a huge black cat of a very unhappy disposition. She snaps and snarls and claws and bites, and Mark Twain takes his turn with the rest; when she gets tired of tearing up manuscript she scratches him and he bears it with a patience wonderful to behold.

———— ••◆•—• ————

With all of this publicity, Bambino became something of a celebrity. In the 1920s and '30s, it was not uncommon for a newspaper to run a feature about Mark Twain's famous cat. The lost-and-found story invariably would be retold, and there probably would be a reference to his proficiency at extinguishing cigar lighters. This was not the end of the celebrity trail for Bambino. He became the co-star of a delightful 2012 children's book, Bambino and Mr. Twain, *written by P. I. Maltbie and illustrated by Daniel Miyares.*

———— ••◆•—• ————

26.

DISCIPLINE "DON'T APPLY" TO A CAT
(from "The Refuge of the Derelicts")

———————

About the same time Bambino went missing and caused such a fuss, Mark Twain was working on a short novel. He never finished "The Refuge of the Derelicts," but it contains this description of the cat.

———————

That's the way with a cat, you know—any cat; they don't give a damn for discipline. And they can't help it, they're made so. But it ain't really insubordination, when you come to look at it right and fair—it's a word that don't apply to a cat. A cat ain't ever anybody's slave or serf or servant, and *can't* be—it ain't *in* him to be. And so, he don't have to obey anybody. He is the only creature in heaven or earth or anywhere that don't have to obey *somebody* or other, including the angels. It sets him above the whole ruck, it puts him in a class by himself. He is independent. You understand the size of it? He is the only independent person there is. In heaven or anywhere else. There's always somebody a king has to obey—a trollop, or a priest, or a ring, or a nation, or a deity or what not—but it ain't so with a cat. A cat ain't servant nor slave to anybody at all. He's got all the independence there is, in Heaven or anywhere else, there ain't any left over for anybody else. He's your friend, if you like, but that's the limit— equal terms, too, be you king or be you cobbler; you can't play any I'm-better-than-you on a cat—*no*, sir! Yes, he's your friend, if you like, but you got to treat him like a gentleman, there ain't any other terms. The minute you don't, he pulls freight.

27.

THE CAT CAME LOAFING IN
(from "The Refuge of the Derelicts")

———————

This passage from "The Refuge of the Derelicts" undoubtedly finds Mark Twain drawing on his own responses to a cat. George is trying to win over a gentleman known as the Admiral. Things aren't going well, until . . .

———————

The cat came loafing in—just at the right time, the fortunate time. George forgot all about the Admiral, and cut his sentence off in the middle, for by birth and heredity he was a worshiper of cats, and when a fine animal of that species strays into a cat-lover's field of vision it is the one and only object the cat-lover is conscious of for one while; he can't take his eyes off it, nor his mind. The Admiral noted the admiration and the welcome in George's face, and was a proud man; his own face relaxed, softened, sweetened, and became as the face of a mother whose child is being praised. George made a swift step, gathered the cat up in his arms, gave him a hug or two, then sat down and spread him across his lap, and began to caress his silken body with lingering long strokes, murmuring, "Beautiful creature . . . wonderful creature!" and such things as that, the Admiral watching him with grateful eyes and a conquered heart . . .

The caressing of the purring cat went on, its flexile body hanging over both ends, its amber eyes blinking slowly and contentedly, its strong claws working in and out of the gloved paws in unutterable satisfaction, the pearl-lined ears taking in the murmured ecstasies of the stranger and understanding them perfectly, and deeply approving them, the Admiral looking on enchanted, moist-eyed, soaked to the bone with happiness.

28.

A CAT'S OPINION ON PAIN
(from *Christian Science*)

*Mark Twain had a keen interest in Christian Science, the religion
founded in 1879 by Mary Baker Eddy.* Christian Science, *a book he
published in 1907, opens with satirical chapters, during which the
badly injured narrator is treated by a Christian Science "doctor." A
cat enters the scene and the discussion.*

Then I thought I would tell her my symptoms and how
I felt, so that she would understand the case; but that
was another inconsequence, she did not need to know
those things; moreover, my remark about how I felt was an
abuse of language, a misapplication of terms.

"One does not feel," she explained; "there is no such thing
as feeling: therefore, to speak of a non-existent thing as existent

is a contradiction. Matter has no existence; nothing exists but mind; the mind cannot feel pain, it can only imagine it."

"But if it hurts, just the same—"

"It doesn't. A thing which is unreal cannot exercise the functions of reality. Pain is unreal; hence, pain cannot hurt."

In making a sweeping gesture to indicate the act of shooing the illusion of pain out of the mind, she raked her hand on a pin in her dress, said "Ouch!" and went tranquilly on with her talk. "You should never allow yourself to speak of how you feel, nor permit others to ask you how you are feeling; you should never concede that you are ill, nor permit others to talk about disease or pain or death or similar non-existences in your presence. Such talk only encourages the mind to continue its empty imaginings." Just at that point the Stubenmadchen trod on the cat's tail, and the cat let fly a frenzy of cat-profanity.

I asked, with caution: "Is a cat's opinion about pain valuable?"

"A cat has no opinion; opinions proceed from mind only; the lower animals, being eternally perishable, have not been granted mind; without mind, opinion is impossible."

"She merely imagined she felt a pain—the cat?"

"She cannot imagine a pain, for imagining is an effect of mind; without mind, there is no imagination. A cat has no imagination."

"Then she had a real pain?"

"I have already told you there is no such thing as real pain."

"It is strange and interesting. I do wonder what was the matter with the cat. Because, there being no such thing as a real pain, and she not being able to imagine an imaginary one, it would seem that God in His pity has compensated the cat with some kind of a mysterious emotion usable when her tail is trodden on which, for the moment, joins cat and Christian in one common brotherhood of—"

She broke in with an irritated—"Peace! The cat feels nothing, the Christian feels nothing. Your empty and foolish imaginings are profanation and blasphemy, and can do you an injury. It is wiser and better and holier to recognize and confess that there is no such thing as disease or pain or death."

"I am full of imaginary tortures," I said, "but I do not think I could be any more uncomfortable if they were real ones."

29.

THE CAT IN
THE CORNER POCKET
(from two letters)

———————•———————

*Still living in Manhattan, Mark Twain escaped the city from May
to October 1907 by renting a house in Tuxedo Park, New York
(about thirty miles away). A little before his return to 21 Fifth Avenue, a little gray cat wandered onto the porch and decided to stay.
"Everybody admires it and thinks it is full of talent," Mark Twain
wrote eleven-year-old Dorothy Quick. They had met a few months
before when both were returning from England aboard the SS Min-
netonka. She became a member of his Aquarium Club, a group of
honorary granddaughters. He encouraged her to write, and she did
indeed become a writer. In 1961, she published* Enchantment: A
Little Girl's Friendship with Mark Twain. *Getting updates about
the little gray cat in Tuxedo Park, Dorothy learned that it brought
them snakes to play with. She also learned he was taking the cat
back to 21 Fifth Avenue. Worried that the cat would be unnamed,*

Dorothy arrived for a visit with a list of possible names. Here's what Mark Twain told her in a 1907 letter.

———————

They're good names. . . . Unfortunately, they're too late for the little cat. She's already christened. It didn't take me long to find a name for her once we'd reached New York. When I discovered she is a terrible scrapper and couldn't be kept in nights, I knew the right and appropriate name for her was Tammany."

———————

Returning for a visit that winter, Dorothy was promised a surprise. She was led into the billiard room.

———————

I opened my eyes, and there was Tammany with four of the most adorable kittens I had ever seen. I dropped to the floor beside the window and gathered two of the little bunches of fur into my arms.

———————

Biographer Albert Bigelow Paine confirmed that Mark Twain "was especially fond" of Tammany. This was the cat the writer referred to when he moved to his last home, Stormfield, in June 1908, saying the cat must be purring on the hearth. At this eighteen-room house near Redding, Connecticut, Tammany soon added to his delight by having another litter of kittens. "We have plenty of cats and kittens now—all descendants of the noble Tammany," he wrote. They were given the run of the house, even being allowed to interrupt Mark Twain's beloved games of billiards. In early October 1908, he wrote the following to Mabel Larkin Patterson, a friend in Chicago.

Mark Twain with a cat crammed into a corner pocket.

If I can find a photograph of my "Tammany" and her kittens, I will enclose it in this. One of them likes to be crammed into a corner-pocket of the billiard table—which he fits as snugly as does a finger in a glove and then he watches the game (and obstructs it) by the hour, and spoils many a shot by putting out his paw and changing the direction of a passing ball. Whenever a ball is in his arms, or so close to him that it cannot be played upon without risk of hurting him, the player is privileged to remove it to anyone of the 3 spots that chances to be vacant.

The family's servant Katy Leary also recalled how the kittens—Sinbad, Billiards, and Danbury—were permitted to scamper about the billiards table.

Mr. Clemens was so fond of cats, and had just as many up at Stormfield as he had in the old days. He had two or three pretty kittens at that time, and they used to jump up on the billiard table when he was playing and shove the balls around and Mr. Clemens, he wouldn't say a word. He just stopped the game and waited patient as could be until they was all through fooling. I remember the name of two of them kittens—one was Sinbad and the other he called Billiards—and he just loved those little things.

———••◆••———

In early November 1908, Mark Twain wrote Dorothy Quick with the sad news that they had "suffered a heavy loss."

———••◆••———

Tammany is dead; killed by a dog, we think, when she was out hunting. She was the finest cat and the handsomest in America. Moreover, she was an officer of the Aquarium. I appointed her myself. She was the Aquarium's MASCAT and brought it good luck as long as she lived. We buried her with the honors due her rank.

———••◆••———

He asked that each Aquarium member wear a black head ribbon for one hour on November 30, which he designated Tammany's birthday (it was his birthday, and the notion of sharing it with a favorite cat delighted him). Dorothy wore the black hair ribbon that day, mourning "that my furry friend was no longer curled up on the hearth." Her descendants, however, continued to rule the Stormfield roost.

———••◆••———

30.

THE SHAKESPEAREAN CAT
(from *Is Shakespeare Dead?*)

Twain didn't go so far as saying Francis Bacon wrote the plays attributed to William Shakespeare, but he believed the evidence pointed that way. He leaned toward the Baconians, and used a cat device to argue the plays must have been written by someone with Bacon's knowledge, experience, and background.

L et me try to illustrate the two systems in a simple and homely way calculated to bring the idea within the grasp of the ignorant and unintelligent. We will suppose a case: take a lap-bred, house-fed, uneducated, inexperienced kitten; take a rugged old Tom that's scarred from stem to rudder-post with the memorials of strenuous experience, and is so cultured, so educated, so limitlessly erudite that one may say of him "all cat-knowledge is his province"; also, take a mouse. Lock the three up in a holeless, crackless, exitless prison-cell. Wait half an hour, then open the cell, introduce a Shakespearite and a Baconian, and let them cipher and assume. The mouse is missing: the question to be decided is, where is it? You can guess both verdicts beforehand. One verdict will say the kitten contains the mouse; the other will as certainly say the mouse is in the tom-cat.

The Shakespearite will Reason like this—(that is not my word, it is his). He will say the kitten may have been attending school when nobody was noticing; therefore we are warranted in assuming that it did so; also, it could have been training in a court-clerk's office when no one was noticing; since that could have happened, we are justified in assuming that it did happen; it could have studied catology in a garret when no one was noticing—therefore it did; it could have attended cat-assizes on the shed-roof nights, for recreation, when no one was noticing, and have harvested a knowledge of cat court-forms and cat lawyer-talk in that way: it could have done it, therefore without a doubt it did; it could have gone soldiering with a war-tribe when no one was noticing, and learned soldier-wiles and soldier-ways, and what to do with a mouse when opportunity offers; the plain inference, therefore, is that that is what it did. Since all these manifold things could have occurred, we have every right to believe they did occur. These patiently and painstakingly accumulated vast acquirements and competences needed but one thing more—opportunity—to convert themselves into triumphant action. The opportunity came, we have the result; beyond shadow of question the mouse is in the kitten.

It is proper to remark that when we of the three cults plant a "We think we may assume," we expect it, under careful watering and fertilizing and tending, to grow up into a strong and hardy and weather-defying "there isn't a shadow of a doubt" at last—and it usually happens.

We know what the Baconian's verdict would be: "There is not a rag of evidence that the kitten has had any training, any education, any experience qualifying it for the present occasion, or is indeed equipped for any achievement above lifting such unclaimed milk as comes its way; but there is abundant evidence—unassailable proof, in fact—that the other animal is equipped, to the last detail, with every qualification necessary for the event. Without shadow of doubt the tom-cat contains the mouse."

Mark Twain, with a porcelain cat in his lap, at Quarry Farm, Elmira, New York, in 1903.
PHOTO COURTESY: THE MARK TWAIN HOUSE & MUSEUM, HARTFORD

PART IV

WHAT IS DEAD CATS GOOD FOR?

One of the most striking differences between a cat

and a lie is that a cat has only nine lives.

—*from* PUDD'NHEAD WILSON

31.

WARTS FOLLOW CAT
(from *The Adventures of Tom Sawyer*)

———————————

"What is dead cats good for?" Tom Sawyer asks the question in the 1876 novel that bears his name. Mark Twain found a variety of uses in several works, starting with this meeting between Tom and his friend, Huckleberry Finn.

———————————

Tom hailed the romantic outcast: "Hello, Huckleberry!"

"Hello yourself, and see how you like it."

"What's that you got?"

"Dead cat."

"Lemme see him, Huck. My, he's pretty stiff. Where'd you get him?"

"Bought him off'n a boy."

"What did you give?"

"I give a blue ticket and a bladder that I got at the slaughterhouse."

"Where'd you get the blue ticket?"

"Bought it off'n Ben Rogers two weeks ago for a hoopstick."

"Say—what is dead cats good for, Huck?"

"Good for. Cure warts with."

"No! Is that so? I know something that's better."

"I bet you don't. What is it?"

"Lemme see him, Huck."

"Why, spunk-water."

"Spunk-water! I wouldn't give a dern for spunk-water . . ."

"But say—how do you cure 'em with dead cats?"

"Why, you take your cat and go and get in the graveyard 'long about midnight when somebody that was wicked has been buried; and when it's midnight a devil will come, or maybe two or three, but you can't see 'em, you can only hear something like the wind, or maybe hear 'em talk; and when they're taking that feller away, you heave your cat after 'em and say, 'Devil follow corpse, cat follow devil, warts follow cat, I'm done with ye!' That'll fetch any wart."

"Sounds right. D'you ever try it, Huck?"

"No, but old Mother Hopkins told me."

"Well, I reckon it's so, then. Becuz they say she's a witch."

"Say! Why, Tom, I know she is. She witched pap. Pap says so his own self. He come along one day, and he sees she was a-witching him, so he took up a rock, and if she hadn't dodged, he'd a got her. Well, that very night he rolled off'n a shed wher' he was a-layin' drunk, and broke his arm."

"Why, that's awful. How did he know she was a-witching him?"

"Lord, pap can tell, easy. Pap says when they keep looking at you right stiddy, they're a-witching you. Specially if they mumble. Becuz when they mumble they're saying the Lord's Prayer backwards."

"Say, Hucky, when you going to try the cat?"

"Tonight. I reckon they'll come after old Hoss Williams tonight."

"But they buried him Saturday. Didn't they get him Saturday night?"

"Why, how you talk! How could their charms work till midnight?—and then it's Sunday. Devils don't slosh around much of a Sunday, I don't reckon."

"I never thought of that. That's so. Lemme go with you?"

"Of course—if you ain't afeard."

"Afeard! 'Taint likely. Will you meow?"

"Yes—and you meow back, if you get a chance. Last time, you kep' me a-meowing around till old Hays went to throwing rocks at me and says 'Dern that cat!' and so I hove a brick through his window—but don't you tell."

"I won't. I couldn't meow that night, becuz auntie was watching me, but I'll meow this time."

32.

CAT CALLS
(from *Adventures of Huckleberry Finn*)

———••••———

Down the river a bit in Adventures of Huckleberry Finn, *Huck and Jim fall in with the Duke and the King, two con artists whose theatrical enterprises are designed to dupe small-town audiences. After being taken in by the conniving pair, several theater patrons from the first two shows in a Mississippi River town return for the third show. Huck is watching the door.*

———••••———

The third night the house was crammed again—and they warn't new-comers this time, but people that was at the show the other two nights. I stood by the duke at the door, and I see that every man that went in had his pockets bulging, or something muffled up under his coat—and I see it warn't no perfumery, neither, not by a long sight. I smelt sickly eggs by the barrel, and rotten cabbages, and such things; and if I know the signs of a dead cat being around, and I bet I do, there was sixty-four of them went in. I shoved in there for a minute, but it was too various for me; I couldn't stand it.

33.

THE NATURALIST TAVERN
(from *A Tramp Abroad*)

The 1878 walking tour of Europe turned into a raft adventure when Mark Twain and his friend returned to Heidelberg by way of river travel. In A Tramp Abroad, *he sarcastically describes the raft crew's response to a storm, with the sea running "inches high." They are saved from "doom" when a man leaps ashore and ties a rope around a handy tree. Mark Twain then tells how they set out in the darkness to find the Naturalist Tavern in the small German town of Hirschhorn.*

W e tramped through the darkness and the drenching summer rain full three miles, and reached "The Naturalist Tavern" in the village of Hirschhorn just an hour before midnight, almost exhausted from hardship, fatigue, and terror. I can never forget that night.

The landlord was rich, and therefore could afford to be crusty and disobliging; he did not at all like being turned out of his warm bed to open his house for us. But no matter, his household got up and cooked a quick supper for us, and we brewed a hot punch for ourselves, to keep off consumption. After supper and punch we had an hour's soothing smoke while we fought the naval battle over again and voted the resolutions; then we retired to exceedingly neat and pretty chambers up stairs that had clean, comfortable beds in them with heirloom pillow-cases most elaborately and tastefully embroidered by hand.

Such rooms and beds and embroidered linen are as frequent in German village inns as they are rare in ours. Our villages are superior to German villages in more merits, excellences, conveniences, and privileges than I can enumerate, but the hotels do not belong in the list.

"The Naturalist Tavern" was not a meaningless name; for all the halls and all the rooms were lined with large glass

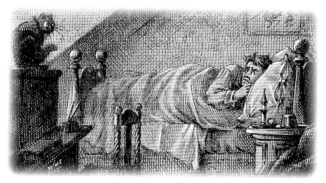

"It was the cat" (illustration for the first edition of *A Tramp Abroad*)

cases which were filled with all sorts of birds and animals, glass-eyed, ably stuffed, and set up in the most natural and eloquent and dramatic attitudes. The moment we were abed, the rain cleared away and the moon came out. I dozed off to sleep while contemplating a great white stuffed owl which was looking intently down on me from a high perch with the air of a person who thought he had met me before, but could not make out for certain.

But young Z. did not get off so easily. He said that as he was sinking deliciously to sleep, the moon lifted away the shadows and developed a huge cat, on a bracket, dead and stuffed, but crouching, with every muscle tense, for a spring, and with its glittering glass eyes aimed straight at him. It made Z. uncomfortable. He tried closing his own eyes, but that did not answer, for a natural instinct kept making him open them again to see if the cat was still getting ready to launch at him,—which she always was. He tried turning his back, but that was a failure; he knew the sinister eyes were on him still. So at last he had to get up, after an hour or two of worry and experiment, and set the cat out in the hall. So he won, that time.

A 1901 *Life* magazine cartoon titled "The American Lion of St. Mark's."

PART V

———— • ————

LIONS AND TIGERS
AND TWAIN

Of all of God's creatures there is only one that
cannot be made the slave of the lash. That one is the
cat. If man could be crossed with the cat, it would
improve man, but it would deteriorate the cat.

—MARK TWAIN, *1894 notebook entry*

34.

THE LION OF ST. MARK
(from *The Innocents Abroad* and
A Tramp Abroad)

Big cats also found their way into Mark Twain's writing. During the Quaker City excursion, he visited Venice. He left behind two descriptions of the Lion of St. Mark, the first in The Innocents Abroad, *published in 1869.*

What would one naturally wish to see first in Venice? The Bridge of Sighs, of course—and next the Church and the Great Square of St. Mark, the Bronze Horses, and the famous Lion of St. Mark. . . . To be on good terms with St. Mark seems to be the very summit of Venetian ambition. They say St. Mark had a tame lion, and used to travel with him—and everywhere that St. Mark went,

A cheerful tiger and lion are among the amused audience in this illustration for
Extracts from Adam's Diary (1904).

the lion was sure to go. It was his protector, his friend, his librarian. And so the Winged Lion of St. Mark, with the open Bible under his paw, is a favorite emblem in the grand old city. It casts its shadow from the most ancient pillar in Venice, in the Grand Square of St. Mark, upon the throngs of free citizens below, and has so done for many a long century. The winged lion is found everywhere—and doubtless here, where the winged lion is, no harm can come . . .

———— ···•··· ————

A more playful description, this of a painting showing St. Mark and the lion, can be found in A Tramp Abroad, *published in 1880.*

———— ···•··· ————

The Lion of St. Mark is there with his book; St. Mark is there with his pen uplifted; he and the Lion are looking each other earnestly in the face, disputing about the way to spell a word— the Lion looks up in rapt admiration while St. Mark spells. This is wonderfully interpreted by the artist. It is the master stroke of this incomparable painting.

35.

LUNCH FOR A LION?
(from *Tom Sawyer Abroad*)

Narrated by Huckleberry Finn, Tom Sawyer Abroad, *published in 1894, is a Jules Verne-like adventure about Tom Sawyer, Huck, and Jim flying across the Atlantic in a mad professor's ship attached to a giant balloon. They eventually reach North Africa and the Sahara Desert.*

W e settled down to within thirty foot of the land,—that is, it was land if sand is land; for this wasn't any thing but pure sand. Tom and me clumb down the ladder and took a run to stretch our legs, and it felt amazing good,—that is, the stretching did, but the sand scorched our feet like hot embers. Next, we see somebody coming, and started to meet him; but we heard Jim shout,

"'RUN! RUN FO' YO' LIFE!'"

and looked around and he was fairly dancing, and making signs, and yelling. We couldn't make out what he said, but we was scared anyway, and begun to heel it back to the balloon. When we got close enough, we understood the words, and they made me sick:

"Run! Run fo' yo' life! Hit's a lion; I kin see him thoo de glass! Run, boys; do please heel it de bes' you kin. He's bu'sted outen de menagerie, en dey ain't nobody to stoop him!"

It made Tom fly, but it took the stiffening all out of my legs. I could only just gasp along the way you do in a dream when there's a ghost gaining on you.

Tom got to the ladder and shinned up it a piece and waited for me; and as soon as I got a foothold on it he shouted to Jim to soar away. But Jim had clean lost his head, and said he had forgot how. So Tom shinned along up and told me to follow; but the lion was arriving, fetching a most ghastly roar with every lope, and my legs shook so I dasn't try to take one of them out of the rounds for fear the other one would give way under me.

But Tom was aboard by this time, and he started the balloon up a little, and stopped it again as soon as the end of the ladder was ten or twelve feet above ground. And there was the lion, a-ripping around under me, and roaring and springing up in the air at the ladder, and only missing it about a quarter of an inch, it seemed to me. It was delicious to be out of his reach, perfectly delicious, and made me feel good and thankful all up one side; but I was hanging there helpless and couldn't climb, and that made me feel perfectly wretched and miserable all down the other. It is most seldom that a person feels so mixed, like that; and it is not to be recommended, either.

Tom asked me what he'd better do, but I didn't know. He asked me if I could hold on whilst he sailed away to a safe place and left the lion behind. I said I could if he didn't go no higher than he was now; but if he went higher I would lose my head and fall, sure. So he said, "Take a good grip," and he started.

"Don't go so fast," I shouted. "It makes my head swim."

He had started like a lightning express. He slowed down, and we glided over the sand slower, but still in a kind of sickening way; for it is uncomfortable to see things sliding and gliding under you like that, and not a sound.

But pretty soon there was plenty of sound, for the lion was catching up. His noise fetched others. You could see them coming on the lope from every direction, and pretty soon there was a couple of dozen of them under me, jumping up at the ladder and snarling and snapping at each other; and so we went skimming along over the sand, and these fellers doing what they could to help us to not forgit the occasion; and then some other beasts come, without an invite, and they started a regular riot down there. . . . Then we sailed off while the fuss was going on, and come down a quarter of a mile off, and they helped me aboard; but by the time we was out of reach again, that gang was on hand once more. And when they see we was really gone and they couldn't get us, they sat down on their hams and looked up at us so kind of disappointed that it was as much as a person could do not to see their side of the matter.

36.

TIGER ON THE FRONT PORCH
(from *Following the Equator*)

———————————

Mark Twain spent more than two months in India during his 1895–96 round-the-world lecture tour. The journey around the globe took a year, yet the chapters about India represent more than one third of the book about this ambitious tour, Following the Equator. *This excerpt is from the chapter recalling his trip from Calcutta to Darjeeling, in the Himalayas.*

———————————

After a while we stopped at a little wooden coop of a station just within the curtain of the somber jungle, a place with a deep and dense forest of great trees and scrub and vines all about it. The royal Bengal tiger is in great force there, and is very bold and unconventional. From this lonely little station a message once went to the railway manager in Calcutta: "Tiger eating station-master on front porch; telegraph instructions."

37.

THE TIGER CUB
(from *Following the Equator*)

———••———

Mark Twain found kittens irresistible, and this passage from his 1897 travel book indicates that the cubs of the planet's biggest cats held the same charm for him. His stay in India also yielded this charming description of a tiger cub.

———••———

I t was there that we saw the baby tiger solemnly spreading its mouth and trying to roar like its majestic mother. It swaggered, scowling, back and forth on its short legs just as it had seen her do on her long ones, and now and then snarling viciously, exposing its teeth, with a threatening lift of its upper lip and bristling moustache; and when it thought it was impressing the visitors, it would spread its mouth wide and do that screechy cry which it meant for a roar, but which did not deceive. It took itself quite seriously, and was lovably comical.

Eve and her pet cats in this illustration from *Eve's Diary.*

Mark Twain writing at the Villa Viviani in Florence in 1892 (notice the little visitor behind his chair in this 1916 illustration for *St. Nicholas Magazine*).

PART VI

———— ·· ————

NO ORDINARY CATS

I simply can't resist a cat.

—*quoted in*

Abroad with Mark Twain and Eugene Field,

BY E. FISHER, *1922*

38.

THE LUCKY CAT
(from "The Chronicle of Young Satan")

Between 1897 and 1900, Mark Twain worked on a novel about Austrian boys visited by a handsome, youthful-looking angel named Satan (a nephew of the original Satan, he is 16,000 years old). This is one of four unfinished manuscripts that have been grouped as "The Mysterious Stranger" stories. Six years after the writer's death, literary executor Albert Bigelow Paine and editor Frederick Duneka published The Mysterious Stranger, A Romance, *presenting it to the world as a complete work by Mark Twain. It was, for the most part, a greatly altered version of "The Chronicle of Young Satan," with the ending of another unfinished work,* The Mysterious Stranger, No. 44, *tacked on as the final chapter. This 1916 publication was exposed as a patched-up work in the 1960s. But Paine and Duneka did not greatly alter the following passages used from "The Chronicle of Young Satan" for their publication,* The Mysterious Stranger. *Mark Twain again finds playful use for the cat. The narrator of "The Chronicle of Young Satan," Theodor, is awed and sometimes perplexed by the charismatic angel named Satan (who tells Theodor to call him Philip Traum). Ursula is the elderly housekeeper for Marget, a young woman in financial trouble.*

———————— ••• • ••• ————————

I was walking along the path, feeling very down-hearted, when a most cheery and tingling freshening-up sensation went rippling through me, and I was too glad for any words, for I knew by that sign that Satan was by. I had noticed it before. Next moment he was alongside of me and I was telling him all my trouble and what had been happening to Marget and her uncle. While we were talking we turned a curve and saw old Ursula resting in the shade of a tree, and she had a lean stray kitten in her lap and was petting it. I asked her where she got it, and she said it came out of the woods and followed her; and she said it probably hadn't any mother or any friends and she was going to take it home and take care of it.

Satan said—"I understand you are very poor. Why do you want to add another mouth to feed? Why don't you give it to some rich person?"

Ursula bridled at this and said: "Perhaps you would like to have it. You must be rich, with your fine clothes and quality airs." Then she sniffed and said: "Give it to the rich—the idea! The rich don't care for anybody but themselves; it's only the poor that have feeling for the poor, and help them. The poor and God. God will provide for this kitten."

"What makes you think so?"

Ursula's eyes snapped with anger. "Because I know it!" she said. "Not a sparrow falls to the ground without His seeing it."

"But it falls, just the same. What good is *seeing* it fall?"

Old Ursula's jaws worked, but she could not get any word out for the moment, she was so horrified. When she got her tongue she stormed out, "Go about your business, you puppy, or I will take a stick to you!"

I could not speak. I was so scared. I knew that with his notions about the human race Satan would consider it a matter of no consequence to strike her dead, there being "plenty more"; but my tongue stood still, I could give her no warning. But nothing happened; Satan remained tranquil—tranquil and indifferent. I suppose he could not be insulted by Ursula any more than the king could be insulted by a tumble-bug. The old woman jumped to her feet when she made her remark, and did it as briskly as a young girl. It had been many years since she had done the like of that. That was Satan's influence; he was a fresh breeze to the weak and the sick, wherever he came. His presence affected even the lean kitten, and it skipped to the ground and began to chase a leaf. This surprised Ursula, and she stood looking at the creature and nodding her head wonderingly, her anger quite forgotten. "What's come over it?" she said. "Awhile ago it could hardly walk."

"You have not seen a kitten of that breed before," said Satan.

Ursula was not proposing to be friendly with the mocking stranger, and she gave him an ungentle look and retorted: "Who asked you to come here and pester me, I'd like to know? And what do you know about what I've seen and what I haven't seen?"

"You haven't seen a kitten with the hair-spines on its tongue pointing to the front, have you?"

"No—nor you, either."

"Well, examine this one and see."

Ursula was become pretty spry, but the kitten was spryer, and she could not catch it, and had to give it up.

Then Satan said: "Give it a name, and maybe it will come."

Ursula tried several names, but the kitten was not interested.

"Call it Agnes. Try that."

The creature answered to the name and came. Ursula examined its tongue. "Upon my word, it's true!" she said. "I have not seen this kind of a cat before. Is it yours?"

"No."

"Then how did you know its name so pat?"

"Because all cats of that breed are named Agnes; they will not answer to any other."

Ursula was impressed.

"It is the most wonderful thing!" Then a shadow of trouble came into her face, for her superstitions were aroused, and she reluctantly put the creature down, saying: "I suppose I must let it go; I am not afraid—no, not exactly that, though the priest—well, I've heard people—indeed, many people . . . And, besides, it is quite well now and can take care of itself." She sighed, and turned to go, murmuring: "It is such a pretty one, too, and would be such company—and the house is so sad and lonesome these troubled days . . . Miss Marget so mournful and just a shadow, and the old master shut up in jail."

"It seems a pity not to keep it," said Satan.

Ursula turned quickly—just as if she were hoping some one would encourage her. "Why?" she asked, wistfully.

"Because this breed brings luck."

"Does it? Is it true? Young man, do you know it to be true? How does it bring luck?"

"Well, it brings money, anyway."

Ursula looked disappointed. "Money? A cat bring money? The idea! You could never sell it here; people do not buy cats here; one can't even give them away." She turned to go.

"I don't mean sell it. I mean have an income from it. This kind is called the Lucky Cat. Its owner finds four silver groschen in his pocket every morning."

I saw the indignation rising in the old woman's face. She was insulted. This boy was making fun of her. That was her thought. She thrust her hands into her pockets and straightened up to give him a piece of her mind. Her temper was all up, and hot. Her mouth came open and let out three words of a bitter sentence, . . . then it fell silent, and the anger in her face turned to surprise or wonder or fear, or something, and she slowly brought out her hands from her pockets and opened them and held them so. In one was my piece of money, in the other lay four silver groschen. She gazed a little while, perhaps to see if the groschen would vanish away; then she said, fervently: "It's true—it's true—and I'm ashamed and beg forgiveness, O dear master and benefactor!" And she ran to Satan and kissed his hand, over and over again, according to the Austrian custom.

In her heart she probably believed it was a witch-cat and an agent of the Devil; but no matter, it was all the more certain to be able to keep its contract and furnish a daily good living for the family, for in matters of finance even the piousest of our peasants would have more confidence in an arrangement with the Devil than with an archangel. Ursula started homeward, with Agnes in her arms, and I said I wished I had her privilege of seeing Marget.

Then I caught my breath, for we were there! There in the parlor, and Marget standing looking at us, astonished. She was feeble and pale, but I knew that those conditions would not last in Satan's atmosphere, and it turned out so. I introduced Satan—that is, Philip Traum—and we sat down and talked. There was no constraint. We were simple folk, in our village, and when a stranger was a pleasant person we were soon friends. Marget wondered how we got in without her hearing us. Traum said the door was open, and we walked in and waited until she should turn around and greet us. This was not true; no door was open; we entered through the walls or the roof or down the chimney, or somehow; but no matter, what Satan wished a person to believe, the person was sure to believe, and so Marget was quite satisfied with that explanation. And then the main part of her mind was on Traum, anyway; she couldn't keep her eyes off him, he was so beautiful. That gratified me, and made me proud. I hoped he would show off some, but he didn't. He seemed only interested in being friendly and telling lies. He said he was an orphan. That made Marget pity him. The water came into her eyes. He said he had never known his mamma; she passed away while he was a young thing; and said his papa was in shattered health, and had no property to speak of—in fact, none of any earthly value—but he had an uncle in business down in the tropics, and he was very well off and had a monopoly, and it was from this uncle that he drew his support. The very mention of a kind uncle was enough to remind Marget of her own, and her eyes filled again. She said she hoped their two uncles would meet, some day. It made me shudder. Philip said he hoped so, too; and that made me shudder again.

"Maybe they will," said Marget. "Does your uncle travel much?"

"Oh yes, he goes all about; he has business everywhere."

. . . And so they went on chatting, and poor Marget forgot her sorrow for one little while, anyway. It was probably the only really bright and cheery hour she had known lately. I saw she liked Philip, and I knew she would. And when he told her he was studying for the ministry I could see that she liked him better than ever. And then, when he promised to get her admitted to the jail so that she could see her uncle, that was the capstone. He said he would give the guards a little present, and she must always go in the evening after dark, and say nothing, "but just show this paper and pass in, and show it again when you come out"—and he scribbled some queer marks on the paper and gave it to her, and she was ever so thankful, and right away was in a fever for the sun to go down; for in that old, cruel time prisoners were not allowed to see their friends, and sometimes they spent years in the jails without ever seeing a friendly face. I judged that the marks on the paper were an enchantment, and that the guards would not know what they were doing, nor have any memory of it afterward; and that was indeed the way of it.

Ursula put her head in at the door now and said: "Supper's ready, miss." Then she saw us and looked frightened, and motioned me to come to her, which I did, and she asked if we had told about the cat. I said no, and she was relieved, and said please don't; for if Miss Marget knew, she would think it was an unholy cat and would send for a priest and have its gifts all purified out of it, and then there wouldn't be any more dividends. So I said we wouldn't tell, and she was satisfied. Then I was beginning to say good-by to Marget, but Satan interrupted and said, ever so politely—well, I don't remember just the words, but anyway he as good as invited himself to supper, and me, too. Of course Marget was miserably embarrassed, for she had no reason to suppose there would be half enough for a sick bird. Ursula heard him, and she came straight into the room, not a bit pleased. At first she was astonished to see Marget looking so fresh and rosy, and said so; then she spoke up in her native tongue, which was Bohemian, and said—as I learned afterward—". . . Miss Marget; there's not victuals enough."

Before Marget could speak, Satan had the word, and was talking back to Ursula in her own language—which was a surprise to her, and for her mistress, too . . . "Didn't I see you down the road awhile ago?"

"Yes, sir."

"Ah, that pleases me; I see you remember me." . . . He stepped to her and whispered: "I told you it is a Lucky Cat. Don't be troubled—it will provide."

That sponged the slate of Ursula's feelings clean of its anxieties, and a deep, financial joy shone in her eyes. The cat's value was augmenting. It was getting full time for Marget to take some sort of notice of Satan's invitation, and she did it in the best way, the honest way that was natural to her. She said she had little to offer, but that we were welcome if we would share it with her.

We had supper in the kitchen, and Ursula waited at table. A small fish was in the frying-pan, crisp and brown and tempting, and one could see that Marget was not expecting such respectable food as this. Ursula brought it, and Marget divided it between Satan and me, declining to take any of it herself; and was beginning to say she did not care for fish to-day, but

Mark Twain's sketch of of a cat, based on an image found on a piece of blue china and described in *A Tramp Abroad*.

she did not finish the remark. It was because she noticed that another fish had appeared in the pan. She looked surprised, but did not say anything. She probably meant to inquire of Ursula about this later. There were other surprises: flesh and game and wines and fruits—things which had been strangers in that house lately; but Marget made no exclamations, and now even looked unsurprised, which was Satan's influence, of course. Satan talked right along, and was entertaining, and made the time pass pleasantly and cheerfully; and although he told a good many lies, it was no harm in him, for he was only an angel and did not know any better. They do not know right from wrong; I knew this, because I remembered what he had said about it. He got on the good side of Ursula. He praised her to Marget, confidentially, but speaking just loud enough for Ursula to hear. He said she was a fine woman, and he hoped some day to bring her and his uncle together. Very soon Ursula was mincing and simpering around in a ridiculous girly way, and smoothing out her gown and prinking at herself like a foolish old hen, and all the time pretending she was not hearing what Satan was saying. I was ashamed, for it showed us to be what Satan considered us, a silly race and trivial. Satan said his uncle entertained a great deal, and to have a clever woman presiding over the festivities would double the attractions of the place.

"But your uncle is a gentleman, isn't he?" asked Marget.

"Yes," said Satan indifferently; "some even call him a Prince, out of compliment, but he is not bigoted; to him personal merit is everything, rank nothing."

. . . My hand was hanging down by my chair; Agnes came along and licked it; by this act a secret was revealed. I started to say, "It is all a mistake; this is just a common, ordinary cat; the hair-needles on her tongue point inward, not outward." But the words did not come, because they couldn't. Satan smiled upon me, and I understood.

39.

NO ORTHODOX CAT
(from *No. 44, The Mysterious Stranger*)

A cat also makes his way into the unfinished No. 44, The Mysterious Stranger. *This was the only work for which Mark Twain himself used "The Mysterious Stranger" as part of a title.*

The cat sat down. Still looking at us in that disconcerting way, she tilted her head first to one side and then the other, inquiringly and cogitatively, the way a cat does when she has struck the unexpected and can't quite make out what she had better do about it. Next she washed one side of her face, making such an awkward and unscientific job of it that almost anybody would have seen that she was either out of practice or didn't know how. She stopped with the one side, and looked bored, and as if she had only been doing it to put in the time, and wished she could think of something else to do to put in some more time. She sat a while, blinking drowsily, then she hit an idea, and looked as if she wondered she hadn't thought of it earlier. She got up and went visiting around among the furniture and belongings, sniffing at each and every article, and elaborately examining it. If it was a chair, she examined it all around, then jumped up in it and sniffed all over its seat and its back; if it was any other thing she could examine all around, she examined it all around; if it was a chest and there was room for her between it and the wall, she crowded herself in behind there and gave it a thorough overhauling; if it was a tall thing, like a washstand, she would stand on her hind toes and stretch up as high as she could, and reach across and paw at the toilet things and try to rake them to where she could smell them; if it was the cupboard, she stood on her toes and reached up and pawed the knob; if it was the table she would squat, and measure the distance, and make a leap, and land in the wrong place, owing to newness to the business; and, part of her going too far and sliding over the edge, she would scramble, and claw at things desperately, and save herself and make good; then she would smell everything on the table, and archly and daintily paw everything around that was movable, and finally paw something off, and skip cheerfully down and paw it some more, throwing herself into the prettiest attitudes, rising on her hind feet and curving her front paws and flirting her head this way and that and glancing down cunningly at the object, then pouncing on it and spatting it half the length of the room, and chasing it up and spatting it again, and again, and racing after it and fetching it another smack—and so on and so on; and suddenly she would tire of it and try to find some way to get to the top of the cupboard or the wardrobe, and if she couldn't she would look troubled and disappointed; and toward the last, when you could see she was getting her bearings well lodged in her head and was satisfied with the place and the arrangements, she relaxed her intensities, and got to purring a little to herself, and praisefully waving her tail between inspections—and at last she was done—done, and everything satisfactory and to her taste.

Being fond of cats, and acquainted with their ways, if I had been a stranger and a person had told me that this cat had spent half an hour in that room before, but hadn't happened to think to examine it until now, I should have been able to say with conviction, "Keep an eye on her, that's no orthodox cat, she's an imitation, there's a flaw in her make-up, you'll find she's born out of wedlock or some other arrested-development accident has happened, she's no true Christian cat, if I know the signs."

40.

A FABLE

(from *The Mysterious Stranger and Other Stories*)

<hr>

A lion, a tiger, a leopard, and a cat figure in this piece that first appeared in a 1922 collection edited by Mark Twain's biographer, Albert Bigelow Paine. The cat, however, gets the final word. We wouldn't have it any other way.

<hr>

Once upon a time an artist who had painted a small and very beautiful picture placed it so that he could see it in the mirror.

He said, "This doubles the distance and softens it, and it is twice as lovely as it was before."

The animals out in the woods heard of this through the housecat, who was greatly admired by them because he was so learned, and so refined and civilized, and so polite and high-bred, and could tell them so much which they didn't know before, and were not certain about afterward. They were much excited about this new piece of gossip, and they asked questions, so as to get at a full understanding of it. They asked what a picture was, and the cat explained.

"It is a flat thing," he said; "wonderfully flat, marvelously flat, enchantingly flat and elegant. And, oh, so beautiful!"

That excited them almost to a frenzy, and they said they would give the world to see it. Then the bear asked:

"What is it that makes it so beautiful?"

"It is the looks of it," said the cat.

This filled them with admiration and uncertainty, and they were more excited than ever. Then the cow asked:

"What is a mirror?"

"It is a hole in the wall," said the cat. "You look in it, and there you see the picture, and it is so dainty and charming and ethereal and inspiring in its unimaginable beauty that your head turns round and round, and you almost swoon with ecstasy."

The ass had not said anything as yet; he now began to throw doubts. He said there had never been anything as beautiful as this before, and probably wasn't now. He said that when it took a whole basketful of sesquipedalian adjectives to whoop up a thing of beauty, it was time for suspicion.

It was easy to see that these doubts were having an effect upon the animals, so the cat went off offended. The subject was dropped for a couple of days, but in the meantime curiosity was taking a fresh start, and there was a revival of interest perceptible. Then the animals assailed the ass for spoiling what could possibly have been a pleasure to them, on a mere suspicion that the picture was not beautiful, without any evidence that such was the case.

The ass was not troubled; he was calm, and said there was one way to find out who was in the right, himself or the cat: he would go and look in that hole, and come back and tell what he found there. The animals felt relieved and grateful, and asked him to go at once—which he did.

But he did not know where he ought to stand; and so, through error, he stood between the picture and the mirror. The result was that the picture had no chance, and didn't show up. He returned home and said: "The cat lied. There was nothing in that hole but an ass. There wasn't a sign of a flat thing visible. It was a handsome ass, and friendly, but just an ass, and nothing more."

The elephant asked: "Did you see it good and clear? Were you close to it?"

"I saw it good and clear, O Hathi, King of Beasts. I was so close that I touched noses with it."

"This is very strange," said the elephant; "the cat was always truthful before—as far as we could make out. Let another witness try. Go, Baloo, look in the hole, and come and report."

So the bear went. When he came back, he said: "Both the cat and the ass have lied; there was nothing in the hole but a bear."

Great was the surprise and puzzlement of the animals. Each was now anxious to make the test himself and get at the straight truth. The elephant sent them one at a time.

First, the cow. She found nothing in the hole but a cow.

The tiger found nothing in it but a tiger.

The lion found nothing in it but a lion.

The leopard found nothing in it but a leopard.

The camel found a camel, and nothing more.

Then Hathi was wroth, and said he would have the truth, if he had to go and fetch it himself. When he returned, he abused his whole subjectry for liars, and was in an unappeasable fury with the moral and mental blindness of the cat. He said that anybody but a near-sighted fool could see that there was nothing in the hole but an elephant.

MORAL, BY THE CAT

You can find in a text whatever you bring, if you will stand between it and the mirror of your imagination. You may not see your ears, but they will be there.

ACKNOWLEDGMENTS

The acknowledgments start with my friend and fellow Mark Twain scholar R. Kent Rasmussen (with whom I've been discussing this cat concept since the late 1990s), agent extraordinaire Charlotte Gusay, and Holly Rubino, senior editor at Lyons Press.

For help with finding the various photographs of Mark Twain with cats, I am deeply grateful to: Melissa Martin, administrative officer at the Mark Twain Papers, located at the University of California's Bancroft Library, in Berkeley; Mallory Howard, the assistant curator at the Mark Twain House & Museum in Hartford, Connecticut; Nathaniel Ball, the archivist and curator at Elmira College's Mark Twain Archive; Rachel Dworkin, the archivist at the Chemung County Historical Society; and indefatigable Mark Twain scholar, collector, and researcher, Kevin Mac Donnell.

Helping to smooth the way to include excerpts from two pieces by Mark Twain was Greta Lindquist, permissions administrator at the University of California Press. For arranging permission to reprint "A Cat-Tale," I am deeply grateful to Richard A. Watson, the lawyer who so ably represents the Mark Twain Foundation. I am also in the debt of many Mark

Twain scholars who have made timely suggestions or cleared the way to precious finds, including Steve Courtney, Robert H. Hirst, Cindy Lovell, Barbara Schmidt, Barbara Snedecor, Mark Woodhouse, and the late Thomas A. Tenney.

Four works more general in their approach to the animal kingdom consulted while assembling this book are: *The Birds and Beasts of Mark Twain* (University of Oklahoma Press, 1966, with original paintings and drawings by Robert Roche), *Mark Twain On Man and Beast* (edited by Janet Smith, Lawrence Hill Books, 1972), *The Higher Animals: A Mark Twain Bestiary* (edited by Maxwell Geismar, Thomas Y. Crowell Company, 1976), and *Mark Twain's Book of Animals* (a handsome and insightful volume edited by longtime Twain friend Shelley Fisher Fishkin, University of California Press, 2010). Three sources for Twain quotes were regularly consulted: Caroline Thomas Harnsberger's *Mark Twain at Your Fingertips* (Beechhurst Press, Inc., 1948), Kent Rasmussen's *The Quotable Mark Twain: His Essential Aphorisms, Witticisms & Concise Quotations* (Contemporary Books, 1997), and Barb Schmidt's amazing website, twainquotes.com.

And to Sara and Becky, who share and understand my mania for Mark Twain and cats, my daily and eternal appreciation for the miracle of their love. Oh, and to the cats who have contributed mightily to my life: the Big Cat, the Little Cat, Dashiell, Pooh, Tigger, Edmund, Eustace, and Poe.

ABOUT THE EDITOR

Mark Dawidziak and Poe, who looks a lot like the cat in the portrait behind them, painted by their friend, artist Susan B. Durkee. *Photo by Becky Dawidziak*

Mark Dawidziak, the television critic at the *Cleveland Plain Dealer*, has written several books on Mark Twain. He has also performed on stage as Mark Twain for more than thiry years.